Ethical School
Leadership

Spencer J. Maxcy

Rowman & Littlefield Education
Lanham • Boulder • New York • Toronto • Plymouth, UK

This title was originally published by ScarecrowEducation.
First Rowman & Littlefield Education edition 2008.

Published in the United States of America
by Rowman & Littlefield Education
A Division of Rowman & Littlefield Publishers, Inc.
A wholly owned subsidary of The Rowman & Littlefield Publishing Group, Inc.
4501 Forbes Boulevard, Suite 200, Lanham, Maryland 20706
www.rowmaneducation.com

Estover Road, Plymouth PL6 7PY, United Kingdom

British Library Cataloguing in Publication Information Available

Library of Congress Cataloging-in-Publication Data
Maxcy, Spencer J.
  Ethical school leadership / Spencer J. Maxcy.
    p. cm.
  Includes bibliographical references (p.) and index.
  ISBN 0-8108-4387-0 (alk. paper)
  ISBN 0-8108-4277-7 (pbk. : alk. paper)
    1. Teachers—Professional ethics. 2. School administrators—Professional ethics.
3. Moral education. 4. Teachers—Training of.   I. Title.

LB1779 .M39 2002
370.11'4—dc21

                                                        2001057691

♾ ™ The paper used in this publication meets the minimum requirements of
American National Standard for Information Sciences-Permanence of
Paper for Printed Library Materials, ANSI/NISO Z39.48-1992.
Manufactured in the United States of America.

For Doreen

Contents

Acknowledgments

While many friends and colleagues, in universities in the United States, Canada, Australia, and elsewhere, have influenced my ideas, some should be named here. Charlie Webber and Tim Goddard of the University of Calgary have both inspired this book and served as careful monitors of the thoughts developed here. Gabriele Lakomski of Melbourne University invited my participation in several Australian projects that stimulated and fueled my search for a more practical educational leadership ethics. John Wilson, formerly of Oxford, inspired me to become practical in my ethics. Bill Foster, Duncan Waite, Fenwick English, Catherine Marshall, Doug Davis, Michael Dantley, Ira Bogotch, and many other scholars have demonstrated how taking the moral and ethical high ground can yield powerful contributions to school leadership. And, finally, former Strongest Woman in the World, Professor Jan Todd of the University of Texas, has served as a model of ethical leadership for our family for many years. She has taught us all how, by holding to the highest values and rising above pettiness and impossible odds, we could succeed beyond our wildest dreams.

To my wife, Doreen, I wish to express my thanks for editing the many drafts that eventually went to make this book you hold in your hands. She has been tireless in her support and encouragement through the toughest of times. And to my daughter Colleen in medical school (who so often sat patiently in coffee shops listening to my theories) and my son Spence in college (who gave up many fishing trips), thanks for teaching me that we must never give up when faced with academic dishonesty, harassment, and other ethical malpractice.

I would like to acknowledge the Louisiana Board of Regents and Mr. Mike Abbiatti for their support of my teaching experiments in distance education.

The catalyst for this book was a grant to develop a distance education course in ethics and leadership for aspiring school principals. This experience enabled me to test out my ideas with graduate students, many of whom taught in school by day but joined me on-line in the evenings and on weekends to explore how to make ethics once again part of educational leading.

Thanks, too, to my LSU colleagues, Abbas Tashakkori, Kim MacGregor, Harriet Taylor, and Dianne Taylor, regarding suggestions for this book.

Finally, I would like to acknowledge my debt to my editor, Thomas F. Koerner, for his patience and encouragement. The production team at Scarecrow made the entire project move smoothly from conception to final product.

1

Ethics, Leadership, and Good Schools

"The quality of leadership is functionally related to the moral climate of the organization and this, in turn, to the moral complexity and skills of the leader."
— Hodgkinson, *Educational Leadership*

Baton Rouge, LA.	"Park Forest principal on leave as cheating allegations probed" Wednesday, March 22, 2000.
Little Rock, AR.	"10 indicted in teacher exam cheating case." Sept. 2, 2000.
New Orleans, LA.	"Former principal of the year booked on extortion charges" Sept. 21, 2000.
Las Vegas, NV.	"Ex-principal arrested with girl, 11, in Nev." May 9, 2001.

Newspaper headlines reveal that there is a crisis in educational leadership today. Many professional educators seem to have lost their way. One announcement after another of unethical or immoral episodes suggest we have a failure in value-oriented practices in our schools. Some professional educators are either ignorant of ethics or seem not to care if they are unethical! To understand what is going on in educational leadership, it is necessary to first examine the nature of the school.

Schools as Moral and Ethical Spaces

Everyone knows what we mean when we speak of a cathedral, shopping mall, art museum, and park. These are places where we go and do things. We pray, shop, view paintings, and stroll in them. These words also distinguish kinds of social spaces (Lefebvre, 1991). For example, the social space of the school is *constructed* (designed, built, furnished, and inhabited) with the goal of being *productive* toward certain ends (learned students, good citizens, career-minded workers, skilled athletes, etc.). The school as a social space also has a *conceptual* and *symbolic* dimension. It contains ideas that take form as lectures, textbooks, and films, as well as images of the school mascot, Drug-Free Zone metal signs, designer clothing logos, and so forth.

Certainly part of what we mean by *school* has less to do with the teaching techniques or scholastic performance of students than with those ideas that make up a kind of coded system of ideas and icons that support the school's operating philosophy. That schools in particular and social spaces in general always exhibit this kind of conceptual and symbolic character is now accepted (Jackson, Boostrum & Hansen, 1993; Starratt, 1994). The ideas and images prized and celebrated by administrators, teachers, students, and staff as well as the physical condition and features of a school are revealing indicators of its values. How the hallways, classrooms, gymnasiums, and principal's office appear indicates what kinds of social relations are valued by the teachers and administrators in that school. The "interior landscaping" of a school is significant where it lends itself to open and frequent positive encounters between and among teachers and students, students and administrators, administrators and teachers, and so on.

When parents visit the school or come into the school building to help in some instructional or social activity, we wonder how they perceive the building. Which symbols of school success are subtly or prominently displayed? Do we see sports trophy cabinets full of gleaming metal? Are the scholars listed with their accomplishments? Do we see photos of principal, teachers, students, and staff? Are examples of student art work displayed in the hallways? Is the atmosphere of the school warm and inviting, or is the school building dark, ill kept, and forbidding? Do we see chains on doors, bars on windows, plywood covering entryways, or alarm boxes?

All of these indicators make up the school *texts*, or stories of the school, showing how administrators, teachers, counselors, staff, and students understand what the school stands for and what defines it. School spaces carry within them meanings of good, bad, right, or wrong. The administrator's vision and mission statements aside, we wish to know what ideas regulate the deportment of the school's inhabitants. Certainly, missions and goals are important and may well reflect this idea network that governs hopes and dreams for the future. But what personal and collective regard does that school elicit from its inhabitants?

Today, schools may be spoken of as diaphanous, having thin veil-like walls that allow elements from the surrounding community, society, and our contemporary culture to penetrate them, while at the same time releasing their students as "products" into the streets to experience and experiment with life. For too long we have focused upon the importance of teaching certain subject matter (math, science, social studies, etc.) and ignored morals and ethics in the curriculum and in our leadership.

Because the school space is permeable and the specific concepts and symbols ingested from the outside culture are technical and rational, we have the current crisis in ethics and leadership. Historically, the schools of this nation and other western nations have rotated through large-scale reforms that set the task of school to be either teaching a certain narrow range of subjects, preparing students for citizenship, educating them to be good social mixers, or preparing them for careers. We have focused our attention in education on national problems such as competing with the Russians to reach the moon or with the Japanese to make more money. Our accomplishments have become short-term fixes, while the question of what we ought to be educating our children for in the future has missed the mark.

Thus, while school is assumed to have a kind of interior moral and ethical landscape (Jackson et. al, 1993) that reflects leadership and how leaders are to lead, that space is also unstable. Our best efforts to date have sought to describe this interior landscape as composed of variables that may be measured relative to their effectiveness in achieving the school mission. Researchers currently hold that schools are environments with workbenches (desks), tools (books and computers), and techniques (methods of teaching), which invariably lead to levels of successful "pupiling." Standardized tests evaluate the degree to which the school has successfully enabled higher performance numbers on these tests. School report cards are fashioned by states and districts to keep parents and teachers apprised of where individual schools are ranked in the effectiveness of their schools.

Such narrow and technical descriptive rankings of the school space leave out the raw elements of difference and division that have bred the conflicts and confusion found there. Because American society has become more diverse and pluralistic over the decades, the school occupies a constructed public space that reflects this in its record. Our democratic form of government and the Civil Rights movement begun in the 1960s contribute to this polyglot nature of school space as well.

Schools operate as a kind of theater or arena for certain key actors—parents, school board members, administrators, teachers, counselors, and others—to engage in activities that are supported and regulated by laws, policies, standards, rules, principles, and norms. As schools have become more complicated, teachers and administrators have also taken on the badge of professionalism. Highly educated and credentialed school leaders today are more apt to be members of the middle class, sophisticated in their use of language and convinced their skills have merit. Driven by the latest educational reforms that call for "high-stakes testing," school report cards, and drawing upon best practices and models of effectiveness to achieve these noble ends, educators are more likely to run into difficulty when dealing with impoverished children and parents who neither share their excellence philosophy nor are driven by professionalism. Members of silent minorities, both parents and students who have been made aware of their repressed conditions want their voices and their rights respected, if not celebrated.

What began as a monolithic educational space in the early nineteenth century, dominated by one culture and one set of values, has moved through phases of cultural pluralism, the melting pot, cultural diversity, cultural identity, and now cultural isolation. Schools are more segregated than ever before, and fewer shared values have a common following. A cultural noise resonates against the rhetoric of national tests, school report cards, and the struggle toward effectiveness.

Ethics and the Search for Quality

"In five minutes you can see what kind of school it is!" reported a State Department of Education official in Baton Rouge, Louisiana. Quality schooling is apparent to the eye. It is no surprise then, that the biggest question facing educational leadership today is how to achieve quality.

To make matters more difficult, quality has many synonyms: We find those who search for quality speaking of it as efficiency, others call it effectiveness, and still others mark it off as achievement. It goes by a host of other names.

But Quality (with a capital Q) is a primary characteristic of life, nature, and experience that appears as an unadorned value, neither measured nor tested. Human beings use their minds and their backs to attempt to know and understand this Quality and to translate it into a multitude of forms in human institutions like schools.

Ancient and modern philosophers in their search to discover what was most important in life separated quality into the good, and the beautiful. The knowledge of good in morals and ethics was considered central to all human living. Recall the Bible and Adam and Eve searching for the knowledge of good and evil.

Appreciation of the beautiful was deemed universally important as well. Witness the ancient Greek and Roman art works that have been left to us. Until the twentieth century, the leading an artfully crafted ethical life and appreciating the beautiful works of human creation were regarded as the highest achievements of the educated person. They also served as the twin principal goals of education.

Yet from the very first, the two notions—one of the good and the other of the beautiful—were gradually unhooked. Over the centuries, the good no longer was connected to the beautiful. During the Middle Ages (500 to 1500), art was held at arm's length from moral and ethical goodness. During the Renaissance, the two came together again in glorious creativity. In the twentieth century, the good and the beautiful were separated once again. For example, the beauty queen may not be a good or moral person in practice. On the other hand, the person dishing up soup to homeless people in the shelter may be less than beautiful but good, moral, and ethical.

Today, in our search for quality in educational leadership, it is vital for us to try to reunite the good (morals and ethics) and the beautiful (creative skill and appreciation) to best fulfill our professional practice. Let us look at why both the moral and ethical and the beautiful may be important to educational leaders.

First, as administrators and teachers we have taken upon ourselves the trappings of a professional life. We have degrees from colleges and universities signifying that we are prepared to practice a set of educational skills—teaching, coaching, counseling, and so forth. Diplomas and certificates, licenses and credentials highlight our commitment to the standards of a profession. Often codes of conduct or standards of practice are set out as models of good practice. These standards of conduct are moral and ethical in nature (although many are based in legal principles as well). There is, then, a substratum of morals and ethics that underwrites how we are to deal with students, parents, and co-educators in the schools.

Next, schools as places may be, as we have seen, either beautiful or ugly. The buildings may be leaking, unclean, and in disrepair, or they may be spaces with clean and bright surfaces that speak of the values of the school. We find ourselves uncomfortable in places that lack the sort of visual qualities we enjoy. On the other hand, these structures may be well designed, repaired, and clean. The hallways may be cheery spaces. Classrooms may be pleasant and warm, with interesting bulletin boards and well-decorated interiors. Creativity is evidenced throughout the space and activities of the school.

Both the good leader and the attractive school participate in Quality. They are linked when an ethical and moral professional educator works in a beautiful, conducive environment. Both the good and the beautiful may operate in unison.

There is another connection between the moral and ethical and the beautiful that we need to consider. The professional educator engages in good work in a regular and systematic way. Professional practice is just that, a kind of repetitive performance marked by moral and ethical indicators. We shall have more to say about these indicators later. Professional educators are living examples of moral and ethical beliefs as reflected in their educational practice.

On the other hand, we must see that the professional educator also exercises judgment. After all, it would not be to his or her credit to perform a moral and ethical act under orders or because of indoctrination without independent thought. Rather, we give credit to the teachers and administrators in a school for being moral and ethical, if and only if they choose to be so and they have an equal opportunity to be otherwise. We call this having free will.

The educator who acts in accord with moral and ethical beliefs on a regular basis and controls his or her actions through judgment and decision may be said to be "composing a life." Like the sculptor or painter, the educator is creating a landscape of teaching and learning, or molding students' future lives. The educator's life is a professional one when it uses the materials and forms of the plastic and performing arts, philosophy, science, literature, and so forth. The raw materials of ideas and experiences form the paint and clay of the creative professional performance.

John Goodlad first alerted us to the status of schools in the United States and the need to pursue the goal of the "good school" in his book *A*

Place Called School (1984). But of late, experts have begun speaking about the good school as a place where ethical and artistic values are easy to detect (Jackson, 1998). Selznick (1992) speaks of certain kinds of collective social groups as examples of "moral commonwealth," a kind of ethically grounded community that gives rise to hope and promise. Campbell (1992) sees such communities rebuilding themselves based upon the principles of usefulness and interest. Beck (1994) tell us that the search for quality is part of the desire to rebuild the school as a finer place. All of these thinkers are motivated by the importance of seeing quality as the means by which we come to see social spaces and to exercise a qualitatively better vision for our lives through the ordinary choices we make.

Often good schooling proposals are cast in narrative form. Terms like *restructuring, effective, efficient* are used instead of images. Subtle translations of text into imaginative snapshots are everywhere. For example, Sergiovanni (1992) reassures us that "the evidence from research on school effectiveness . . . and school culture . . . increasingly suggests that effective schools have virtuous qualities that account for a large measure of their success (p. 99)." Statistically relevant concepts (e.g., effective) re-place the image of virtuous praxis.

Educational administration scholars are so committed to their research methods that few are willing to try out new images or redescriptions. Thus, we find the same old methods cited as yielding "statistically significant" truths about moral and ethical leadership practice and school reform. Educational leadership becomes a reflection of past theoretical frameworks and mind-sets as well as the rationalization of present practice: all text based rather than image specific.

The upshot is that what is known about ethical leadership and what is understood about it are vastly different. Narrow research studies using ultrasophisticated methodologies on small numbers of leaders and schools, or large-scale reviews using these small-scale investigations, yield the same thing: very few ideas that a school leader can implement to make for better ethical decision making.

If contemporary school reforms are something of a spectacle, it is the kind of spectacle that reoccurs. "School choice" advocates sound like Horace Mann. The essential details may differ, but the moralistic jargon and moral realism remain. School reform has become high theater, with superintendents and school boards fighting it out on cable television. So image driven is this spectacle that we cannot locate answers or redemption in the techno-scientific language of standard educational research reports. The words fail to capture the color and vibration of the scene. The result is that parents and school reform followers are lulled into assuming that what is said is what is seen.

The idea of the good school is cloaked in a variety of proposals for school reform that seem to pivot on conceptions of the institutional good, where *institution* is equated with *school*, and *good* is equated with *effective, productive, achievement oriented*, and so on (Finn, 1991). However, in the past, a good school was rarely seen as the moral or ethical school, a place where students learned how ethics affected their decisions. This tendency to identify good with productive value, and moral-ethical with humanistic value, has been corrected by some recent researchers in educational administration (Jackson et al., 1993; Murry, 1995; Roy, 1996). Jackson and colleagues demonstrated that morals and ethics were overt as well as subtle and pervasive aspects of classrooms. Murry's (1995) research found that being a moral leader in an urban school translated into a number of different strategies. Roy discovered that the "moral elementary school" was both explicitly and implicitly moral. A study of principals by Roy (1996) examined principals' values as expressed in disciplinary acts. She found that principals communicated moral and ethical values in a myriad of actions, from greeting students in the morning to rearranging the furniture in the lounge. In these studies, the good school comes into view as a unique kind of community where individuals are bonded by moral and ethical values.

Despite these groundbreaking studies, the tendency remains for researchers to reduce good schooling to financially frugal schooling. The good school, to be the virtuous school, must be structured around cost-effectiveness. Teachers and administrators, qua leaders, are assumed to be stewards of the good, moral monitors of the educational community now seen as a kind of religious organization. It is their task to serve, respect and to establish and retain shared values. Unfortunately, this means the good school is viewed as the effective school, and leadership is elevated into a transcultural norm and practice of ministering the holy word. We have not come very far from Ellwood Patterson Cubberley's school manager as Puritan.

Determining the good in education, whether as an orchestrated set of teaching strategies or a vision of a planned school organizational configuration, has serious implications for students, parents, teachers, and administrators. Out of these alternative conceptions of good schooling has arisen a variety of reform efforts, like the search for educational excellence, school restructuring, effective schools reforms, and so forth, which have occupied civic attention and drawn down financial resources. It is not entirely clear, however, whether such reform submovements have any potential importance in raising our consciousness regarding the place leadership or ethics occupies as guiding norms in educational change. Rather, such subreforms are typically attached to assumed organizational configurations that are both modernist and positivist in architecture and processes.

As Beyer and Liston (1992) point out, "one of the prerequisites for any sort of social transformation is a moral and political vision of how things might be different and better . . ." (p. 389). Unfortunately, the current direction in educational reform is to mask the moral and ethical image of a good school and to push to the front a rationale for technical mastery over costs. If it is dangerous to subsume the moral and ethical reform of schools under religious redemption, it is equally wrong to subsume it under financial cost-cutting. This is to clothe a moral argument in economics garb.

Finally, the desire to shuck it all and simply return to the pleasures of the hearth and home is also a dead end. Hearn (1997) tells us that today the problem does not reside in withdrawing into private life to search for a "morally dense solidarity," in strong families and vibrant neighborhoods, but rather it is in "the deterioration of private life as a place set apart from the social capital destroying forces of modernity (p. 132)." Any emphasis on retreat, say to home schooling, from the communal space of institutions like schools, makes individual rights without social obligations an unsatisfactory and impractical solution. Leadership disappears behind a philosophy of "right."

In the final analysis, good schools are fluid and structured containers holding the ongoing record of tough value choices and the residual moral and ethical character of their leaders and members.

Being an Ethical Leader: Knowledge, Dispositions, and Skills

In the chapters to follow, we shall explore what moral and ethical leaders need to know and understand about ethics and leading, what dispositions or attitudes they require to act ethically, and how they can make more skilled moral and ethical decisions in their professional work. In the chapters to follow you will discover how to sort through the rhetoric of hype and educational boosterism and the confusing claims upon schools and resources that result from our pluralistic and decentered society. The fundamental goal is helping you make practical moral and ethical decisions. The three-part requirement used here (knowledge, dispositions, acts) is prompted by the Interstate School Leadership Licensure Consortium's (ISLLC) "Standards for School Leaders" published in 1996. In this report, the authors set out six standards by which to gauge school leadership. These standards (one of which covers ethics) call for leaders to have knowledge, dispositions, and performances match the standard. The division of professional practice into these three categories requires enlargement and elaboration, however. In the chapters to follow, we shall discover how school leaders can become better practical decision makers, with particular reference to morals and ethics. We will explore and expand upon the notion of *standard* and show you how to move beyond the standards to improve the quality of teaching, learning, administration, and other aspects of your school.

Knowledge and Understanding

As educational leadership has become more complicated and moral and ethical problems more difficult, experts have stressed that we therefore need to have more knowledge. Yet this claim is incomplete: more understanding is needed as well. After we have acquired all the facts, we must also understand how to be ethical and moral, have a model of leadership to guide us, and use good decision-making skills. More than the knowledge of facts is required. We must understand the sources of moral and ethical dilemmas, what makes human beings tick, how schools function as social organizations, and so forth. More than knowing, we must understand what philosophers have taught us about ethics, which leadership approach is most prone to succeed, and a host of other matters in order to be able to actually make practical ethical decisions.

Ethical leadership is moral and ethical because leading requires that we understand human nature and relations. *Star Trek*'s Data and Mr. Spock were nonhuman life or half-human forms who struggled to decipher human transactions because they seemed so illogical. It is precisely because our passions, desires, and interests are not logical, but rather value centered, that they may be seen as truly human.

Unless we understand morals and ethics as more than mere talk, and less than the most finely hewn theory, we miss the entry point to successful resolution of so many contested issues in education. For example, school leaders must deal with proposals calling for school prayer. Those who blindly follow the legal characterization of prayer in schools run the risk of upsetting the moral and ethical (religious) beliefs of some of the students and their parents who disagree. As a result, the school climate is eroded, and leading becomes impossible. On the other hand, to accede to every moral and ethical interest claiming school space may lead to the embrace of cults engaged in devil worship or suicide pacts. Seeing these as alternative societal members pledged to radically different takes on the world allows us to draw upon the criteria of art and the test of aesthetic value in making our judgments.

We must also understand that we may fail. In evaluating a contested situation, leadership must be capable of making a mistake of interpretation. For example, if leadership is called upon to decide who is morally or ethically right or correct, there must be a range of possible answers based upon differing moral and ethical points of views and theories. Not to know such differing moral and ethical perspectives leaves leaders open to the charge that they cannot understand the present dilemma and cannot make a fully informed decision.

Values and Facts

The school leader must know about Quality or the moral and ethical domain itself to be a good ethical leader. To be sensitive to Quality is to comprehend the value network that makes up the climate or context, culture or space of the school. Prevailing values define the school.

The facts of particular moral and ethical problems and issues also need recognition and understanding. The ethical leader must be sensitive to the evidence, opinions, and other matters that bear on the case.

Theories of Ethics

When faced with a moral and ethical dilemma, a school leader should first know or understand the appropriate moral and ethical theory for solving the problem. Moral philosophy has gone through four historic stages. Begun in ancient Greece and continuing into the sixteenth century, the authoritarian stage found most people believing that moral and ethical ideas came from outside human nature. The second stage began with Michel de Montaigne and the publication of *Essays* (1595) and culminated in the philosophy of Immanuel Kant and Jeremy Bentham. This orientation held that the source of moral decisions must be found within free and self-governing human nature. The third stage stretched from the eighteenth century into the twentieth. Here philosophers elaborated and defended the proposition that each person has free will and is responsible for his or her moral and ethical choices. The current stage of moral philosophy has begun to shift from the problems associated with the autonomous individual to a concern for public morals and ethics (Schneewind, 1991).

All moral and ethical theories deal with: (1) what is good, and (2) what is the *right* thing to do. Moral philosophers have historically emphasized the origins, status, and components of good; ethical philosophers have stressed the right and wrong features of choices. This distinction does not always hold true, so the tendency in more recent philosophy has been to speak of both as philosophers of *value*.

Two other orientations have divided moral and ethical philosophy. Some philosophers focus upon *rules* and constraints upon persons making moral and ethical choices. This orientation is called deontological. For the deontologist, the most important consideration is the norm, rule, or principle that regulates human action. If a person knows the rule, he or she is obligated to act in terms of it. For example, if I know that telling a lie is wrong, I am obligated to tell the truth under all circumstances. This may create some problems. Consider the teacher who was held up; the robber demanded to know where her money was—and she told him!

Another group of philosophers have given primary attention to the *consequences* or results of moral and ethical actions. This orientation is referred to as teleological, or more commonly consequentialist. For the consequentialist the major consideration is that the moral and ethical decision maker consider the impact or results of his or her decision. In addition, for whatever values a person or institutional leader (administrator, teacher, student, or staff member) adopts, the correct response is to promote them. Consequentialism is teleological and covers a number of ends-oriented philosophies, most prominently utilitarianism and naturalism.

A variety of specific and unique variations on these themes have led to the following list of approaches to ethics that have been used in the past. Each of these schools of thought has been popular during different periods of history. In future chapters, we shall explore these schools of thinking, called traditionalism, realism, utilitarianism, emotivism, subjectivism, and naturalism. The views associated with naturalism will be used in this book because they are currently the most widely held and because John Dewey, the first significant philosopher of American education, appealed to them in his views of schooling, views that have had enormous impact over time.

Quite simply, naturalism holds that moral and ethical decisions are made in natural situations—settings and conditions that are ordinary yet vested with controversy. The methods we may use to solve moral and ethical dilemmas should be both scientific and creative (artistic). The test of our decision will be its effect on the situation (making things better or worse). No external agencies or authorities need be appealed to in "doing ethics." The consequences reveal the adequacy of our decision and provide a guide to future decisions.

Leadership Theories and Models

David Hemsath (2001) talks of "toxic leadership" in the workplace. This style of leading has invaded the schools as well. Educational leaders with deadly values can poison creativity, and ultimately the good-making characteristics, of organizations. Schools have begun embracing theories and models of leadership which cast principals, teachers, counselors, students, and parents in the role of enforcers and duty sergeants. Education has abandoned the norms of caring and creativity in exchange for the narrower, stifling values of efficiency and effectiveness. And these values have been extended from children to parents to business owners and community leaders. Accountability has been introduced into a national system of schools already stressed to their limits and struggling with increased violence and discipline problems. Targets and goals have been set, making an additional percentage point on a school's "report card" a life-or-death matter. To avoid having the school placed in receivership or having teachers and the principal moved to other schools, educators have chosen to alter test scores, prompt students with the correct answers, and teach for the high-stakes tests, all in an effort to gain praise and avoid blame.

It is sometimes said that we live in an era of leadership vacuum. If there is a crisis in our schools today, that crisis is made worse by the absence of good leadership. School administrators and teachers are often not prepared to understand the ethical dilemmas they face or to deal with them. This was not always the case. As school administration rose in stature to be considered a teachable craft in the first two decades of the twentieth century, school leaders were expected to be "managers of virtue" (Tyack & Hansot, 1982). The principals were well grounded in values through their own elementary and secondary school training, family up-bringing, and situation in the community. Americans expected school administrators to be models of the virtues they held dear.

The expectation that school leaders would also be moral and ethical leaders gradually collapsed as school administration took on more of the trappings of a science. University preparation programs shifted to the assumption that all that was required for "training" school principals was a thorough grounding in scientific fact. By the 1920s and 1930s educational leadership preparation and practice became dedicated to effectiveness and efficiency. The school leader was to be trained in accounting and managerial skills (Callahan, 1961).

Leadership Theories   Leadership theories have followed the trends in administrator training over the years and may be lumped into three types: During the first part of the twentieth century, leadership was taken to refer to *human traits*; with the discovery of behavioral psychology, leadership was considered to be *behavior*; and, when these two approaches were deemed too narrow to capture its essence, leadership was considered to be *situational*. As you might expect, the shift from traits of character, in which moral values held center stage, to leadership as merely behavior saw an accompanying disappearance of moral and ethical preparation in the principalship. When leading is a product of one's situation, it is even less likely that moral character and virtue will be part of the leader's preparation.

Leadership in a moral and ethical situation requires us to be aware of the views we and other people have about leadership. Since we focus on the setting and the social space of the school, we are necessarily looking at the transactions between people. To settle a moral and ethical dilemma, a transactional understanding of leadership requires less than transforming the situation or characters involved. Some changes may occur, but we shall maintain that the sort of change agent Badiou (2001) speaks about, a radical innovator, is probably neither necessary or desirable. On the other hand we shall see that a Machiavellian leader who simply maintains his or her power and the status quo of the institution, at the expense of others, is not acceptable either.

What we have come to understand during the research on educational leadership is that it is a multisided concept. Yes, it may be important to have certain traits of *character* to lead well, and you need to behave in such a way that you provide a *model* of good practice for others to follow. Leadership is different in different situations. Not all schools are the same, so no one model of leadership will work in every situation. We ought to be *adaptive* in our leadership approach, gearing our leading to the situation.

Finally, we must know or understand some things about human nature and the social space of the school, and we must have the required skills to think and act in a moral and ethical manner.

Leadership Models   More important than these gross distinctions among scholarly studies of leadership is the existence of leadership models. Differing modes of leading, or "leadership styles," are most readily adopted by school administrators and teachers. Among the models we shall investigate will be charismatic leadership (leading through personality), bureaucratic leadership (leading through dependability), servant leadership (leading through service), transformational or radical leadership (leading by changing), and reflective leadership (leading through intelligence). Each of these models has different characteristics and makes different demands upon the educator. Each impacts the decision-making process in moral and ethical cases.

Dispositions

In practicing any craft, we must also have certain dispositions or attitudes toward our actions. The ancient philosophers referred to these attitudes as virtues. To be ethical meant for them that one had a particular disposition to act in a certain way. For example, if you possessed the virtue of fairness, you would treat people fairly. If you had an honest disposition, you would act honestly in dealing with a moral and ethical choice.

In ethical leadership, many dispositions or virtues are available. We will learn about a number of these. Justice and caring are two dispositions that command much attention today. In addition, there are others such as being considerate of people's rights, acting in terms of the common good (of the school), wishing to do least harm, having courage, being temperate or prudent, and being honest.

When these virtues or dispositions are acted upon, they form what is called the moral character of the person. When one's virtues outnumber the vices, and seem to work in harmony, we tend to speak of a person having "integrity." Our aim in this book is to help the reader to learn about dispositions of a moral and ethical kind (virtues) and how to exercise them in making choices, so as to build one's moral character. The sum total of our dispositions to act ethically and morally is our moral character. School leaders who lead their schools with moral character help provide a model of ethical behavior for every student, teacher, staff member, and parent associated with that school.

Skills of Moral and Ethical Decision-Making

It is important to see leadership ethics as connected to decision making. If a leader knows and understands what is involved in a moral and ethical case, is disposed to act in a moral and ethical manner, and yet fails to decide skillfully in the case, his or her moral character fails to be developed and the situation is made no better.

There are twin paths to sound decision making, one through the methods of science and the other through the creativity associated with the arts. Both come together as an interwoven "criticism of criticism."

Scientific Skills

John Dewey stated, "Ethics is the science that deals with conduct . . . [and] aims to give a systematic account of our judgments about conduct, in so far as these estimate it from the standpoint of right or wrong, good or bad" (Dewey & Tufts, 1908/1932, p. 3). So began John Dewey's effort to place ethical study on a scientific basis and to set it within a dynamic early twentieth century culture and its institutions.

Dewey attempted to take the dusty old theories of ethics and rework them, fashioning a "naturalistic" depiction of what amounted to ethical experience in his time. At the heart of Dewey's plan was a root practical philosophy that focused upon education as "doing" and the results of practice.

Ethical problem solving may benefit from the scientific skills of analysis and guided observation available from the social sciences. We shall be looking more carefully at the scientific side of moral and ethical decision making in the chapters ahead. It is enough at this point to say that moral-ethical decision making profits from a *scientific attitude* in which the problematic situation is inquired into, possible facts are located, hypotheses or possible solutions are considered, and so on. However, it is also important to understand that we do not have a science of ethics. The domain of quality and ethics is so vast and imprecise, and the social impacts on leadership so numerous and difficult to detect, that a science has not emerged.

Artistic Skills

"Good educational leadership is a creative art." All of our forms of art—painting, sculpture, dance, music—are central to human life, and their creation and enjoyment set us apart from other creatures. Thus, if understanding is our goal (with all its measures and tests), we should be open to what part art forms may play in our achieving knowledge and truth. Art may be a path to understanding the lens science and technology have provided on morals and education, now and in the future.

Artistic skill pivots on creativity. The capacity to think in original or unique ways is important in artistic work. Creating new solutions, composing new options, rehearsing strategies, and locating tools to resolve dilemmas better—all of these are exercises in creative thinking.

In art, essentially, we must begin and end with Quality. The universe is dynamic and changing. This dynamism is like certain nodes of experience that characterize it, from a supernova in outer space, to the child opening a birthday package. What is attached to each and every occurrence is Quality, or a kind of unadorned value. Before the scientist looks through the telescope, and before the parent snaps the photo of the birthday child, the experience holds this characteristic of value.

Art and ethics are really quite close. For centuries, philosophers have told us that art helps in transforming human life, lifting us up from the petty and mundane to a level of existence that is ennobled. The goal of art is to help us live our lives as if they are works of art, or as Mary Catherine Bateson (1989) put it, "composing a life," by which she means using the skills of thinking and creativity to fashion a life that is good to live.

When we turn our critical eye upon those experiences which may lead to better living, we may prize or condemn them. But in either case we express an evaluation. To judge an experience is to engage in a kind of *appraisal*. Here we look for the worthwhile features of the experience and how they relate to one another and to the future.

Once we have evaluated the experience, we may change our plans for the future, or we may change our future experience. When we appraise the alternative routes we may take, selecting one because of certain criteria and overall likely outcomes and impacts, we return to Quality. Our decision is a good one, if it turns out.

Ethical educational leadership is both a scientific and artistic form of problem solving. It is a criticism of criticism, in the sense that it is a set of thinking tools that themselves undergo refinement through practice.

Conclusion

This book seeks to show you how to make sound moral and ethical decisions in your capacity as a school leader. The specific goals of this text are to (1) help you know and understand the qualitative nature of the school and culture (2) point to resources, both theoretical and practical, to help you deal with moral and ethical dilemmas in your leading, and (3) demonstrate how to refine your decision-making skills to make your choices more fruitful and your work easier.

In the chapters to follow we will explore the major themes that contribute to developing a practical ethical leadership. Chapter 2 will discuss the "leadership standards" and what impacts they are having on educational leadership and particularly on moral and ethical decision making. Chapter 3 explores the meanings of ethical leadership and their significance for schools and morals and ethics. In Chapter 4 we examine the ways in which people become moral and ethical. Chapter 5 and Chapter 6 look at justice and caring as dispositions. Chapter 7 investigates the relationship of science to leadership and ethics. Chapter 8 provides a template for moral and ethical decision making seen as reflective practice. In the appendixes are found cases for further study and skill development. Throughout the text, you will find the emphasis is on demonstrating the linkage between leadership and ethics, and on the knowledge, understandings, dispositions, and skills needed to help you make sound moral and ethical decisions, and thus to promote and sustain a good school.

2

Standards and Ethics

*"A people that values its privileges above
its principles soon loses both."*
— Dwight D. Eisenhower,
Presidential Inaugural Address, January 20, 1953.

Within the past decade, new leadership standards have appeared on the school scene as definitions of what it means to be an effective leader. While these standards are an effort to make some progress against the leadership vacuum felt in public institutions, they pose a particular challenge for the school leader. The new standards for school leaders have emerged as a set of legislated guidelines in many states and regulate entrance into the profession and the practice of school principals. Additionally, school leaders face the daunting task of helping students in their schools comply with the new standards of performance as measured by high-stakes tests.

Performance Standards in Education Today

All professions have explicit and implicit standards that gauge the quality of their craft. In the past, these benchmarks were visible cuts into the wooden bench a craftsman used to create a product and were visible dimensions by which a particular performance could be measured. Gauges and standards go hand in hand, so measurement is an inevitable result of having a standard. A few centuries ago, the British royalty had certain tradesmen who they patronized. Bread was baked by a baker who displayed the royal standard above his shop door, for example. This idea of a symbol of excellence came to be widespread. If we see *USDA* on a piece of meat in the freezer in the super-market, we believe it denotes a certain level of quality—which presupposes that some meat did not meet the standard.

Standards seem to lend a layer of comfort to our exchanges with people. If a standard is abided by, for example in water for drinking, we feel comfortable in consuming or using that substance or service. Quality is guaranteed at some level.

It is quite natural that we would wish to see professionals like doctors, dentists, and educators perform their labor at some level of acceptability. A standard of performance allows us the confidence to use or employ such people. This insurance is somewhat misleading, however. We may have a low standard that marks minimal safety levels for human consumption and therefore use products that are marginally safe. Meanwhile, the truly excellent products or services are not noted or touted. Minimal standards do not help us improve the quality of our institutions or products and lead to marginally acceptable performances. Therefore, one of the problems with standards is the "threshold problem," or the fact that to be widely deployable a standard must be more average than exceptionally good. From an ethical and leadership perspective, we see that standards are capable of reducing the quality of leadership.

Another difficulty with standards is that they may curb experimentation and creativity. Conformity to the standard is valued over deviance from it; trying new things is not encouraged. After all, leaders who experiment and take chances may fail. Failure is what standards seek to eliminate. Success is offered via the safe route: Do it the way everyone else does and you will be guaranteed success.

The source of standards is important as well. The leadership standards for educators came from focus groups and surveys of practicing school administrators. In a sense, the best practice was the average practice of average professionals. Instead of developing models of the most successful practice, the standards advocates drew on the average practitioner. This is not to say that the average leader is not a good leader. Rather, it points once again at the mediocrity trap that has emerged. Leadership standards must be easy to specify and easy to mimic. The ease with which they are achieved and then the repetitive nature of meeting the standard all lend themselves to humdrum leadership and ultimately to ineffective leading.

Leadership standards are available in the history books but seem to have eluded the standards-bearers in educational administration. Leadership theories drawing upon historic examples such as Napoleon, Gandhi,

Thoreau, and so on, are available and may be used to set higher standards for leaders today. We should think in terms of greatness and not merely average qualities and performances, values and ideals. If we do not, the standards will soon be outdated because every administrator will have a crib sheet with which to mimic the labor that should go into meeting any standard. Teaching for the standards will invade colleges and departments of education and leadership. We will level down the entire enterprise while satisfying the accountability experts who dislike differences.

The formalistic movement for leadership standards for school administrators sits between the actual performances of principals on the one side, and a collection of moral and ethical dispositions that inform these performances on the other. It is quite easy to neglect the moral and ethical side of these performances, assuming instead that all we need are "the facts." But facts are nothing without quality, and determining the kind or type of qualitative judgment needed is a challenge.

Finally, the thirst for standards by which to judge leadership performance implies that leaders are actors or performers and the responsibility of managing and guiding a school is nothing but a drama. Instead of being dedicated and immersed in the school, the principal is a stage actor who enters and exits the theater of statewide education, competing with the other actors in educational reform, and contributing to the overall entertainment of the effects. As Arons (1997) tells us, the standards-driven educational reforms have eroded our sense of face-to-face school community. School leaders are playing for the larger audience of state and national critics.

In this chapter we will examine the standards by which school leaders are to be held accountable, as well as the role of standards in testing students and schools in the United States. We will compare the attitude toward standards as measures of effectiveness with the belief that all one needs is moral and ethical sensitivity to be a leader. These cases find challenging moral and ethical dimensions that inform the use of the standards relative to the real world situations the prospective school leader will face, yet are not reducible to mindless pronouncements or buck-passing.

What Are Standards and Principles?

By their very nature, standards and principles are rough measures or benchmarks of acceptable performance. They are unlike laws and policies, which are narrow and specific pronouncements about a range of expected practices and behaviors within specific settings and exercises of choice, and are often accompanied by strong administrative or judicial consequences if they are broken or unheeded. Standards and principles are norms or rough guidelines for acceptable practices that can be used to measure the performance of students, teachers, staff members, or anyone else in a school.

Standards are expressions of someone's values. They call upon us to attend to them, to exercise judgment about the match between activities and the standard. It is expected that if the action does not match the standard, we are to work toward improving our performance relative to the standard. Improvement may entail simply trying harder, or being improved through some kind of educational or training experience.

Standards and principles are rough expressions of hope. For example, it may be that the school board has accepted a standard of performance for band members that includes such things as dressing in the band uniform, bringing one's instrument to the football game, and marching in unison with other members of the band. It hopes that, for the sake of the band, or the school, each band member will adhere to the standard. The overall appearance of the band and its ability to command public respect, win band competitions, improve attendance at football games, and so on makes this particular standard worthwhile as a regulative norm.

On the surface, there would seem to be little of ethics involved in these correlations of standard to practice per se. But attached to every standard or principle is a select and quite foundational collection of assumptions about a variety of matters (Fish, 1999). Standards and principles are not value neutral pronouncements that originate either in Heaven or in our democratic way of life (to give but two long-standing efforts to tether principles and standards of behavior to religious or political philosophies).

If we look carefully at such standards as fairness, impartiality, mutual respect, or reasonableness, for example, we find that these principles assume at least two things: (1) They assume they are neutral as benchmarks and favor no particular person or group of persons, but rather respect everyone; and (2) they also assume "a way of life," or "the way things ought to be" (Fish, 1999, p. 1–3).

Thus, when we put such standards into operation, they carry with them an agenda (often hidden) that guides people toward engaging in certain kinds of value-free judging and some end state assumed to be worthwhile (Fish, 1999). The principle of treating students fairly in a school assumes some things about the human mind and thinking. For example, it may be taken for granted that a school leader will be totally objective in his or her decisions in cases involving the standard. It supposes that the leader has a kind of rationality or wisdom that allows him or her to rise above petty personal beliefs or emotional behavior in making a judgment.

The principle of treating students fairly in a school assumes background conditions for schooling (e.g., that a school is a place like home, or teaching has a family-oriented structure). The schoolhouse is taken to be a certain kind of space filled with the things that allow the standard to be followed and lead to a more efficient or more effective educational institution.

Standards and principles are supposed to be free of any commitments to an agenda. For example, a school leader should not punish a student for not wearing her band uniform sash to Saturday night's football game, while also believing that football is the biggest source of outside revenue for the school and that uniformity of dress impresses those who donate money to the athletic fund. From the standards philosophy currently operative in education, such a substantive commitment could never be attached to adhering to the standard. But it often is! School leaders make decisions that are weighted either implicitly or explicitly in favor of certain substantive goals and groups over others.

Standards that profess to be neutral regarding race, gender, class, religious persuasion, ethnicity, sexual orientation, and so on cannot be neutral. In today's schools, these substantives are the heart and soul of education. We cannot profess that we are treating students fairly if we cannot also treat some more favorably than others. For example, students with identified special needs have the law on their side. A school principal must treat those students differently from the mainstream or be held accountable by the court. Fairness is to give preference to the student with special needs—more teacher attention, special accommodations in the classroom, school bus changes, and so forth. The result is that value-neutrality is pure public relations and lacks any connection with the actual conditions that regulate decisions.

The Standards Movement in School Administration

The so-called standards movement in educational administration has swept the United States by storm. A number of professional associations and societies are engaged in creating, evaluating, and discriminating "standards" by which the leadership behaviors of school leaders are to be measured. It is assumed that these performance standards may be taught to novice administrators as guides for future professional practice.

After two years of labor in crafting a set of standards for school leaders, on November 2, 1966, the Interstate School Leaders Licensure Consortium (ISLLC), a program of the Council of Chief State School Officers (state superintendents throughout the United States), adopted the Standards for School Leaders (see table 2.1). ISLLC and the standards writers had close affiliations and connections with other educational groups, and dialogues with the Educational Testing Services (ETS) resulted in the creation of a test for school leaders. The group was also influenced by several national reports calling for

---

Table 2.1 ISLLC Leadership Standards

Standard 1: A school administrator is an educational leader who promotes the success of all students by facilitating the development, articulation, implementation, and stewardship of a vision of learning that is shared and supported by the school community.

Standard 2: A school administrator is an educational leader who promotes the success of all students by advocating, nurturing, and sustaining a school culture and instructional program conducive to student learning and staff professional growth.

Standard 3: A school administrator is an educational leader who promotes the success of all students by ensuring management of the organization, operations, and resources for a safe, efficient, and effective learning environment.

Standard 4: A school administrator is an educational leader who promotes the success of all students by collaborating with families and community members, responding to diverse community interests and needs, and mobilizing community resources.

Standard 5: A school administrator is an educational leader who promotes the success of all students by acting with integrity, fairness, and in an ethical manner.

Standard 6: A school administrator is an educational leader who promotes the success of all students by understanding, responding to, and influencing the larger political, social, economic, legal, and cultural context.

[Adopted by the Council of Chief State School Officers, November 1994 and published in 1996]

---

the reinvention of leadership for tomorrow's schools. The aim was to enhance school leaders' skills and to link educational leadership to *effective* education.

While the ISLLC group had hoped to stimulate dialogue among people involved with school administration, they also sought to encourage professional educational associations and agencies to adopt the standards they had created. They hoped that this would start the ball rolling and promote the adoption of the standards or variations on the theme of the standards within state educational agencies and legislatures in each state.

A much deeper aim was to transform school administration into effective leadership. Historically, school administrators had typically been regarded as managers. A spate of literature beginning in the 1960s attempted to cast school administrators as leaders. This research and policy promotion had been accepted by many professors of educational administration in colleges and universities but was largely ignored by the rank-and-file educational bureaucracies. In order to advance the valued research that school administration professors had published, it was reasoned that school principals and superintendents needed to be taught leadership skills. Since educational administrators were not evaluated on their efforts to remake their schools, but rather to maintain quality education, such injunctions failed.

School principals were to be tested and licensed! While the justification for such a move was rooted in the changed nature of society, with poverty being the pivotal issue, in fact the movement for leadership standards was an effort to introduce a new set of gatekeeping functions into educational administration.

Guiding Principles

The standards for school leaders were to reflect the centrality of student learning, acknowledge the changing role of the school leader, recognize the collaborative nature of school leadership, and provide a means to upgrade the quality of the education profession. It was taken for granted that the standards would be used to inform testing companies, in particular Educational Testing Service (ETS), of what the new tests for licensing school administrators should test for (i.e., performance of school leaders).

The ISLLC standards aimed to identify three things educational leaders could be held accountable for: (1) the knowledge, (2) dispositions, and (3) performances a leader would manifest in professional practice. These standards were used by the individual states as a model for constructing their own standards for leaders.

Standard 5: The Ethics Standard

There is no doubt that the ISLLC standards have been the most influential in moving educational administration to a standards-based model. Six standards were specified by the original model, each with a list of knowledges, dispositions, and performances required of the school administrator. While all of the standards were fairly straightforward, Standard 5 (the ethics standard) was different. Standard 5 was spelled out as: "A school administrator is an educational leader who promotes the success of all students by acting with integrity, fairness, and in an ethical manner" (http://www.ccsso.org/standards.html).

Table 2.2 ISLLC Standard 5: The Ethics Standard

Knowledge	**The administrator has knowledge and understanding of:** • various ethical frameworks and perspectives on ethics • the purpose of education and the role of leadership in modern society • the values of the diverse school community • professional codes of ethics • the philosophy and history of education
Dispositions	**The administrator believes in, values, and is committed to:** • the ideal of the common good • the principles in the Bill of Rights • the right of every student to a free, quality education • bringing ethical principles to the decision-making process • subordinating one's own interest to the good of the school community • accepting the consequences for upholding one's principles and actions • using the influence of one's office constructively and productively in the service of all students and their families • development of a caring school community
Performances	**The administrator:** • examines personal and professional values • demonstrates a personal and professional code of ethics

Table 2.2 ISLLC Standard 5: The Ethics Standard *continued*

- demonstrates values, beliefs, and attitudes that inspire others to higher levels of performance
- serves as a role model
- accepts responsibility for school operations
- considers the impact of one's administrative practices on others
- uses the influence of the office to enhance the educational program rather than for personal gain
- treats people fairly, equitably, and with dignity and respect
- protects the rights and confidentiality of students and staff
- demonstrates appreciation for and sensitivity to the diversity in the school community
- recognizes and respects the legitimate authority of others
- examines and considers the prevailing values of the diverse school community
- expects that others in the school community will demonstrate integrity and exercise ethical behavior
- opens the school to public scrutiny
- fulfills legal and contractual obligations
- applies laws and procedures fairly, wisely, and considerately

The Principal's View of the Ethics Standard

In a study of principals conducted in Louisiana, investigators sought to discover which of the seven standards for school leaders adopted by the state were most valued by practicing school principals, and whether or not these principals thought they needed development in any of the standards (Maxcy, Tashakkori & Iwanicki, 1999). The author and two colleagues focused upon the efforts of one state (Louisiana) to reform school principals' professional practice. In order to develop performance standards for practicing as well as new school principals, a task force of principals, teachers, and other educators had been convened in 1997–98 by the Louisiana Department of Education. The result was the development of seven standards along with forty-seven performance indicators. The intent of the standards development effort was to provide a framework for principal preparation and development at the parish and district level. A statewide validation study of the standards and performance indicators was conducted (Tashakkori & Iwanicki, 1998). Findings from this investigation led to many interesting conclusions.

One of these seven standards was ethics. There were eight performance indicators for professional ethics: (1) model ethical behavior at both the school and community levels, (2) communicate to others expectations of ethical behavior, (3) respect the rights and dignity of others, (4) provide accurate information without distortion or violating the rights of others, (5) develop a caring school environment in collaboration with the faculty and staff, (6) apply laws, policies, regulations, and procedures fairly, consistently, wisely, and with compassion, (7) minimize bias in self and others and accept responsibility for one's own decisions and actions, and (8) address unethical behavior in self and others.

When principals were asked to rank each of the seven standards in terms of its degree of importance for their own professional success, principals surprised the investigators. Overall, the standard of professional ethics was ranked first (of highest importance) by the greatest majority (71%) of the principals surveyed. The next highest ranked standard was school management (60%). Although the principals surveyed were asked to rank only one of the standards as the highest in importance, some principals assigned a rank of 1 to more than one standard. Despite this limitation, results clearly revealed that practicing principals preferred and were concerned with professional ethics.

Yet, even though the principals thought ethics was the most important standard for their craft, they did not see any strong need to receive training in it. When it came to identifying the need for professional development, the performance indicators relating to professional ethics had the lowest average! (A comparison of male and female principals indicated that the female principals perceived professional ethics to be slightly more important than did the males, a trend that was also present for other standards. On the other hand, they expressed a lesser need for professional development in professional ethics.)

Thus, this study showed that school principals by a large percentage included among the most important professional ethics performance indicators for their professional success. This finding deserves special researcher attention, because little attention currently is paid to these performances in the training of aspiring principals, and despite its perceived importance, the principals apparently believe that they do not need much additional training in professional ethics.

There are several possible explanations for these trends. One may be that since most people believe ethical values are acquired in the normal course of growing up, school principals assume they import such norms into their professional work. Therefore, they see no need to become a part of professional development activities or programs that will teach them to be ethical in their leadership.

A second explanation may be that principals do not wish to admit they require assistance from others in dealing with ethical dilemmas in their schools because to do so is to admit they either lack ethics or do not know how to use it in decision making. Baumeister (1998) describes this situation by saying, "people typically believe that they are superior to the average person or to various other targets, and so when they compare themselves to other people (or to an abstract average) they feel quite good about themselves" (p. 685).

The third explanation may be that principals simply feel they have received enough experience in being moral and hence training in ethics as a part of credentialing or other schooling is a waste of time. Beck and Murphy (1994) see this belief tacitly accepted by university and college professors who give lukewarm treatment to ethical issues in preparing principals.

There are probably other explanations, but those offered here all have direct implications for principal preparation and professional practice. In the light of the relative criticism of the degree of preparation and ability of principals for dealing with professional ethics, perhaps future professional preparation and development efforts should focus on the inconsistencies between perceptions and the actual need for professional ethics in practice (Beck, 1994). Attention given to ethical choice in the new standards may be a genuflection in the proper direction, but unless the principals are aware that they may have problems in dealing with ethical dilemmas, emphasis on the importance of ethics may not necessarily lead to actual changes in practice. Creating an awareness of possible areas of weakness in these performances should be an essential part of any training and professional development program for principals (Maxcy, Tashakkori & Iwaniki, 1999).

What Does the Principal Have to Know about the Ethics Standard to Do a Good Job?

For administrators striving to become ethical leaders of their schools or education units, ISLLC Standard 5, the so-called ethics standard, is of prime importance. Here we have specified what one must know and desire to do in the realm of ethics, plus the indicators in practice that will be used to test them. The ethics standard can be used as a super standard to work through all the other standards and to put them into practice in the most moral and ethical way. The ethics standard is the standard by which the others may be measured.

A closer examination of the ISLLC Standard 5 reveals a number of assumptions about what will count as ethical leadership on the part of the school principal:

Know about Ethics. Standard 5 tells us that the ethical school leader ought to have knowledge of ethics and where to get that knowledge. Most importantly for our purposes, this knowledge includes understanding the frameworks and perspectives of ethics, codes of ethics, the purpose and role of leadership in modern society, and the philosophy and history of education, which provides such knowledge. The ethical leader ought to know the diverse values in her school.

Understand Rights and the Common Good. Standard 5 speaks about "the common good," while also telling school leaders they must be committed to the Bill of Rights. Here we see that two attitudes, one that looks at the larger impact of ethical decisions on the school space and its members, and the other that looks to the individual and his or her rights. The school leader ought to decide which must be stressed in a particular case

Use Ethics in Decision Making. There is a need to see ethics within the ordinary decisions school leaders make in schools. This sensitivity, we must assume, is often lacking in contemporary school administration.

Accept Responsibility for Decisions. Interestingly, Standard 5 reattaches responsibility to decision making. In the past, school administrators have sought to make the institution, school board, or other agencies the bad guy. Now the ISLLC group refocuses responsibility on the school leader.

Develop a Caring School Community. Standard 5 also tells the school leader to be caring and compassionate. We see the framers of the standards embracing caring and individual rights as well as justice and fairness.

Have a Personal and Professional Code of Ethics. First, we see that an ethical leader will perform in certain ways by demonstrating that he or she has examined personal and professional values and shows a personal and professional code of ethics. It is assumed that there are personal moral and ethical values and codified moral and ethical values that leaders can use in their work. The ethical leader ought therefore to seek out examples of these personal and professional ethical codes. By reading biographies of great leaders who expressed high standards of ethics in their lives, we may formulate a personal set of ethics. In addition, we may wish to visit the codes of ethics for educators that are part of professional associations' documents. The National Education Association (NEA) (http://www.nea.org/aboutnea/code.html), National Association of Elementary School Principals (NAESP) (http://www.naesp.org/ethics.htm), and other groups that focus on school leadership are excellent sources for model codes of ethics that may form the basis of your own code (see tables 2.3 and 2.4).

Table 2.3 National Education Association Code of Ethics of the Education Profession

Preamble

The educator, believing in the worth and dignity of each human being, recognizes the supreme importance of the pursuit of truth, devotion to excellence, and the nurture of the democratic principles. Essential to these goals is the protection of freedom to learn and to teach and the guarantee of equal educational opportunity for all. The educator accepts the responsibility to adhere to the highest ethical standards.

The educator recognizes the magnitude of the responsibility inherent in the teaching process.

The desire for the respect and confidence of one's colleagues, of students, of parents, and of the members of the community provides the incentive to attain and maintain the highest possible degree of ethical conduct. The Code of Ethics of the Education Profession indicates the aspiration of all educators and provides standards by which to judge conduct.

The remedies specified by the NEA and/or its affiliates for the violation of any provision of this Code shall be exclusive and no such provision shall be enforceable in any form other than the one specifically designated by the NEA or its affiliates.

PRINCIPLE I: Commitment to the Student

The educator strives to help each student realize his or her potential as a worthy and effective member of society. The educator therefore works to stimulate the spirit of inquiry, the acquisition of knowledge and understanding, and the thoughtful formulation of worthy goals.

In fulfillment of the obligation to the student, the educator—

1. Shall not unreasonably restrain the student from independent action in the pursuit of learning.
2. Shall not unreasonably deny the student's access to varying points of view.

3. Shall not deliberately suppress or distort subject matter relevant to the student's progress.
4. Shall make reasonable effort to protect the student from conditions harmful to learning or to health and safety.
5. Shall not intentionally expose the student to embarrassment or disparagement.
6. Shall not on the basis of race, color, creed, sex, national origin, marital status, political or religious beliefs, family, social or cultural background, or sexual orientation, unfairly—
   a. Exclude any student from participation in any program
   b. Deny benefits to any student
   c. Grant any advantage to any student
7. Shall not use professional relationships with students for private advantage.
8. Shall not disclose information about students obtained in the course of professional service unless disclosure serves a compelling professional purpose or is required by law.

PRINCIPLE II: *Commitment to the Profession*

The education profession is vested by the public with a trust and responsibility requiring the highest ideals of professional service. In the belief that the quality of the services of the education profession directly influences the nation and its citizens, the educator shall exert every effort to raise professional standards, to promote a climate that encourages the exercise of professional judgment, to achieve conditions that attract persons worthy of the trust to careers in education, and to assist in preventing the practice of the profession by unqualified persons. In fulfillment of the obligation to the profession, the educator—

1. Shall not in an application for a professional position deliberately make a false statement or fail to disclose a material fact related to competency and qualifications.
2. Shall not misrepresent his/her professional qualifications.
3. Shall not assist any entry into the profession of a person known to be unqualified in respect to character, education, or other relevant attribute.
4. Shall not knowingly make a false statement concerning the qualifications of a candidate for a professional position.
5. Shall not assist a noneducator in the unauthorized practice of teaching.
6. Shall not disclose information about colleagues obtained in the course of professional service unless disclosure serves a compelling professional purpose or is required by law.
7. Shall not knowingly make false or malicious statements about a colleague.
8. Shall not accept any gratuity, gift, or favor that might impair or appear to influence professional decisions or action.

[Adopted by the NEA 1975 Representative Assembly]

Table 2.4 National Association of Elementary School Principals Code of Ethics

National Association of Elementary School Principals
Statement of Ethics for School Administrators
NAESP Policy Statement 1100.3

An educational administrator's professional behavior must conform to an ethical code. The code must be idealistic and at the same time practical, so that it can apply reasonably to all educational administrators. The administrator acknowledges that the schools belong to the public they serve for the purpose of providing educational opportunities to all. However, the administrator assumes responsibility for providing professional leadership in the school and community. This responsibility requires the administrator to maintain standards of exemplary professional conduct. It must be recognized that the administrator's actions will be viewed and appraised by the community, professional associates, and students. To these ends, the administrator subscribes to the following statements of standards.

1. Makes the well-being of students the fundamental value in all decision making and actions.
2. Fulfills professional responsibilities with honesty and integrity.
3. Supports the principle of due process and protects the civil and human rights of all individuals.
4. Obeys local, state, and national laws.
5. Implements the governing board of education's policies and administrative rules and regulations.
6. Pursues appropriate measures to correct those laws, policies, and regulations that are not consistent with sound educational goals.
7. Avoids using positions for personal gain through political, social, religious, economic, or other influence.
8. Accepts academic degrees or professional certification only from duly accredited institutions.
9. Maintains the standards and seeks to improve the effectiveness of the profession through research and continuing professional development.
10. Honors all contracts until fulfillment or release.

[Adopted by the NAESP Board of Directors, September 29, 1976]

Serve as a Role Model for Ethics. Standard 5 supports the importance of school principals serving as a role model of ethical leadership. It is stated that one must "inspire others" and use the influence of the principal's office to enhance programmatic goals (rather than personal gain). We are led to believe that the ethical school leader leads a moral and ethical life in the school (and outside), and this image should have a positive impact on the school.

We have been saying that ethics is a practical matter, and Standard 5 bears this out. Everything about Standard 5 is aimed at practice. However, while Standard 5 seeks to place its feet firmly on the ground of practice, it also has its eyes to the heavens. Each of the statements in Standard 5 has an unannounced theoretical basis. Our task in this book is to illuminate the theories that regulate ethical practice.

Things to Watch for in Leading from the Standards

The Standards and Social Justice. As Dantley and Cambron-McCabe (2001) tell us, the ISLLC standards for leaders do not have much to say directly about social justice. The principal's major duties are to maintain and improve test scores and yet not speak about making schools more democratic or equitable. Thus, if you are hoping to be a transformational leader seeking to introduce more just and equitable conditions into your school for pupils or teachers, you may not find much support in the standards or see your efforts in the test of your performances.

The Standards Minimize Ethical Leadership. Despite the fact that the ISLLC Standard 5 addresses ethics, we find it to be vague on the historical and theoretical sources for ethics. We are not told the sources of the particular ethical values that are to be valued by the leader. We are not instructed in how ethical decisions are to be made. And we are not more knowledgeable about how ethics can be used to promote the good of the school and the people within its space. Ethics is viewed as a straightforward implementation of ethical knowledge. Unfortunately, ethics is not like physics. In Western nations there are no ethical laws that regulate the conduct of human beings and their social spaces.

Martha M. McCarthy and Khaula H. Murtadha (2001) conclude from their study of the reception of ISLLC standards and ETS licensure in Indiana that standards-based leadership is welcomed. However, citing English (2000), Foster (1986), and Maxcy (2000), they tell us that standards-based leadership and principal tests will reduce the amount of attention of a critical kind given to school practices, inequalities, diversity issues, and so on. The focus on technical outputs, like student test scores, "de-emphasize school leaders as moral leaders."

No Call for Critique or Recognition of New Dilemmas. The tendency in the standards is to repress or push aside root problems in North Carolina, Catherine Marshall (2001) tells us. There is an almost naive assumption that all the issues and controversies are known. The leader must merely be energetic to lead more effectively regarding them. But leadership is affected by dilemmas, and dilemmas are affected by leadership. Change and the new problems emerging in schools require a way in which these standards may be improved and their power controlled via critical and reflective thinking. Where there is no critique, standards and principles become encrusted with tradition and practice becomes ritualistic and ineffective.

Standards and Licensure Testing. As noted above, a national test of leadership was created by ETS and placed on the market at a cost of approximately $200. The standards were quickly connected to the accountability side of education. Testing had been sweeping the American landscape for some years, with a number of states adopting statewide tests for student promotion, commonly called high-stakes tests, in the grades.

As Peter Sacks (2001) tells us, standardized tests have led to "standardized minds." There is today a national obsession with measurement and testing. Historically, students were evaluated within each classroom relative to their classmates. The so-called bell-shaped curve allowed pupils to be compared with one another in small groups of thirty or so students. That history yielded an orgy of testing that led to larger-scale exams like the SAT, ability grouping, programs for gifted learners, and now national accountability of all students as favored by President George Bush. This desire to know how each child measures up to national standards has had the result of making parents suspicious of their own child's abilities. The mythical "average performance" creates a sacred ideal that does not exist while it forms doubt and uncertainty about the adequacy of every child, teacher of that child, and administrator of the child's school if he or she falls below the norm.

At the heart of these state and national tests are standards with accompanying validated indicators of effective performance. Standardized tests have bred accountability, or the questioning of why the bottom-scoring half of the U.S. school population is less adequate than the top half! These indicators will be tested against the character choices made by the players in our scenarios. Readers may test their own decisions and rationales against the author's.

In this increasingly testing-conspicuous age, we are witnessing a narrowing of the role of school administrative decision making. While concern for standards of professional administrative performance is acknowledged, it is assumed by educational experts that increased research methodological sophistication alone will yield needed (verifiable) student achievement effects. The view is often further embellished by the dogmatic belief that teaching refined inquiry methods to school administrators in university school administrator preparation programs is all that will be needed to achieve effective schools in the future.

Moral Character and Standards-Based Leadership Decisions

The leader who engages in a moral and ethical choice regarding one of the standards of professional practice, like the school leadership standards, should be knowledgeable about the circumstances in which the decision will be made, free to choose among two or more options, and able to include that choice as consistent with and a part of his or her moral character. The moral character of the leader is involved in every moral and ethical decision made in a school. We have seen that standards are evaluated in terms of whether or not the practicing leader has demonstrated a disposition, or state of mind. Each attitude toward a moral and ethical action forms a piece of what we shall call a leader's character.

It should be no surprise, then, that leadership character would be developed over time through the exercise of choice. As habits of consideration and practical reflection are built, the character of the human being becomes formed. The leader's moral and ethical character is how he or she conducts himself or herself relative to choices. A leader with experience and training in making moral choices must adopt certain attitudes and dispositions (virtues) that are reinforced through practice. This is the way to develop moral character, and this character may help in the dark hours of moral and ethical decision making encountered in educational leadership.

It is reasonable to assume that a leader who lies, cheats, or steals is ill-suited to the demands of exercising choices about honesty, deception, or theft. There is something to be said for learning about the virtues of good moral and ethical living, exercising the virtues in real world situations, as a preparation for moral leadership as a school administrator, teacher, counselor, or school board member.

Principals are held accountable for the performance of teachers and students in their school. As part of the recommended set of skills principals ought to possess, that of developing a vision is paramount. In earlier times, the principal could get by on budgeting, scheduling, and other mundane talents. Today' principals must have a vision, or a plan for the school, that tells what its objectives are in the way of preparing students for living.

Too often, we assume a leadership vision to be the result of one's imagination. But the vision may most often come from one's planned approach to dealing with a crisis. The vision can function as a step-by-step design; a template or blueprint for action. These descriptors need not require imagination. They may be copies, or forms of imitation of others' visions and the strategies to achieve them.

When a vision is thought to be imaginative, it may originate in the mind of one individual or may be a collective result of many persons. The first kind of imagined future relies upon the creative energy of one individual. For example, we may say of the principal that the school vision is a result of her imagination. However, once formed, the vision must be communicated to the teachers (and parents). Finally, the others "buy into" the vision and begin working toward it.

Quite another process may be used to arrive at a vision. This process is more democratic and starts in a grassroots way. Teachers and parents form vision statements, students provide visions, and board members or others may communicate visions. These are gathered up and the principal in consort with teachers and parents, students, staff, and community members details the vision as a conjoint understanding.

Visions are fine, but they require some basis in fact. A vision that calls for an inner-city school to operate like an elite private prep school may not be well founded in the cultural and social facts of the situation.

The experience of the group would be invaluable in the work of framing a vision statement for a school.

The Impact of Ethical Decisions on School Spaces

The second direction a standards-based leadership takes is toward the social space of the school. As we have seen, moral and ethical decisions made by the principal both defines his or her moral character and forms a code of professional and personal conduct. However, once these decisions become part of the human dynamics of the school, they redefine the moral and ethical space of the school.

Shared Decision Making

We cannot stress any more firmly the value of sharing decision making with teachers, parents, and pupils as their interests come into play.

Jocelyn A. Butler and Kate M. Dickson (1987) identified the need to establish a leadership team and involve staff members in school improvement. The school culture became the announced centerpiece of reform. They reasoned that increased collaborating, cooperation, and collegiality were needed if efforts to improve the school were to work. A leadership team allowed teachers to work together in decision making to move the school through the improvement plan. Teachers were directly involved with the school improvement leadership.

The principal and leadership team restructured the ways in which faculty and administration communicate with each other. Faculty governance and regular meetings between faculty and administration were instituted. Setting a schoolwide improvement goal and involving all staff in deciding the focus for school improvement became paramount. At Centennial High School, three key expectations emerged:

1. Improvement efforts were of high priority, to be ongoing and driven by the results of effective schools research.
2. Staff could and should be involved in school improvement efforts.
3. The focus of school improvement was to improve student performance.

What is interesting about Centennial High's school improvement plan was that it was not focused upon the school culture but rather on the school structure and the power relationships in the school. Strong leadership with a flow of information from administration to staff was emphasized. While learning was deemed important, it was instructional effectiveness that mattered. Only one variable in the plan spoke at all about the cultural environment as needing to be "pleasant." The structure of the organization was paramount.

Improving Schools Morally and Ethically

Nigel Bennett and Alma Harris (1999) argue that school effectiveness and school improvement researchers have made efforts to establish some kind of dynamic relationship between their respective fields without success. School effectiveness research views organizational change in terms of structural change, while school improvement research sees such success coming from the cultural dimensions of organizational change. These two views result in a methodological and theoretical separation that has proved difficult to bridge, the authors argue. They suggest power may be the catalyst to link school structure and effectiveness with school culture and improvement.

Rather than power, what is required is moral and ethical leadership attached to a vision of the school as a moral and ethical space. Schools cannot be effective or improve if the leadership of the school lacks moral character. Where the school leader lies and cheats, uses the office for personal gain, or in other ways operates in morally and ethically reprehensible ways, the school space is affected. Schools cannot be moral or ethical places when leaders are unethical and immoral themselves.

A Moral and Ethical Decision-Making Structure: Standards and Consequences

Educators as moral leaders of their schools ought to use good judgment in their work. There are basically two ways to do this: by focusing upon each individual case relative to the standard, or by looking at the likely consequences of the decision.

This text has proposed using practical judgment in such decisions. There are two strong pulls and pushes on school leaders as they engage in this practical decision making: they must consider the standards of their profession as well as the likely outcomes stemming from these standards-warranted choices.

Standards

Philosophers speak of moral and ethical decisions that take seriously rules, gauges, and standards as driven by deontology. When a leader makes a choice in which a rule, policy, or standard is the considered factor, he or she is engaging in a deontological ethics, or ethical decision making governed by rule or law.

The philosopher Kant made the study of standards-based decisions his philosophical centerpiece. For Kant, one rule or standard rose above all others. To paraphrase Kant, "So decide that your decision could be made a rule for all people." Introducing an abstract principle that operates as a universal standard is not new. We find the ancients invoking us to "do unto others as they do unto you." Jesus challenged his followers to "turn the other cheek." The Ten Commandments are examples of abstract principles that are to be used to regulate daily affairs. As such these standards are rules for proper performance.

These high-minded principles seem to be taken for granted in many school situations. Children will often fight, because "he hit me first." The first standard requires us to think of our actions in terms of whether others in a similar situation could make the same choice, and whether that choice would do less harm than others.

School leaders must be quite careful not to tie a kickback to their decisions. The school principal who received a grant to do a project, entrusted aides and teachers to perform the activities outlined in the grant, and paid them for their labor in keeping with the grant was morally and ethically correct. When she demanded a kickback of several hundred dollars from these people, she violated the ethics of the grant and she broke the law.

Consequences

A second approach to moral and ethical decision-making assessment calls for us to look at the consequences of our decision, both anticipated and real.

The utilitarians, a group of philosophers who fastened upon results as the test of moral and ethical decision making, have perhaps most affected the American context. Here the test of whether the decision is a good one or not is the result that would stem from it. For example, if a school leader knows that the father of a child who is expelled will beat the child severely, the leader should consider the consequences of this option versus an in-school suspension where the father would not beat the child.

There are two kinds of utilitarians: act utilitarians and rule utilitarians. An act utilitarian considers only the probable consequences of an action. For example, if a kindergarten teacher weighs discipline of a student for using a toy as a weapon against the possible results this might have on the child, she would be using an act utilitarian method. If, however, she were to weigh the impact of disciplining a child upon the entire class, all of whom were children of soldiers stationed nearby, she would be engaging in a rule utilitarian decision-making strategy. She would be concerned with her action if it were seen as a rule for others in the future.

Good Schools: Understanding the Substantive Assumptions in Standards-Based Decisions

It is vital that the ethical leader understand the substantive assumptions underwriting the standards and principles she or he is charged to uphold. The benchmarks of successful performance as a leader or as a student operate in much the same manner. Each standard begs the question of what it means for the person evaluated and the significance of the project of which she or he is a part. The teacher who is held to a standard of performance in teaching math or history is playing a role in a much larger drama: the way of life of a school. It is central to every performance that evaluation that the leader consider how the actions fit in with the vision of the school, where it is going, and what effects are garnered for students.

Recently, a superintendent of a rural school district in a southern state came under severe criticism. His fourth and eighth graders fared poorly on the state tests designed to signal promotion to the next grades. He criticized the performance of the elementary school children and chided the parents and teachers for not preparing them better for the exams. The parents suggested he was expecting too much from the students. An aura of mistrust of the leader was pervasive.

When these students put on a play in the school auditorium soon after the test scores were received, this superintendent remarked publicly that it was "poor" in quality and the students would have better spent their time working to get their math grades up for the next round of high-stakes testing. Parents revolted. They sought to remove the superintendent, calling him insensitive and without feeling. They believed that their children were learning by putting on the play. It did not have to be Broadway quality to be educationally significant!

The school leader soon shifted gears. In a plan he called "Blueprint for Better Schools," this superintendent stressed that what was needed was a vision of what school was for. "We want them (graduates) to be really prepared for life after high school, whether it's college, vocational school, or a job in the real world" (Fryer, 2001, 9B). School system officials visited local businesses and industries to learn what they need in the way of workers and how students might best be prepared for those jobs. The teaching of "the work ethic" was proposed. Time in the new "technical centers" will provide opportunities to develop skills ranging from auto mechanics to computer tech. A math and science center will prepare students in these areas. At the heart of this plan is the view that schools must establish a correlation between the classroom and the rest of life (Fryer, 2001). Rather than the short-term goal of preparing children for high-stakes tests, educators are rededicating the school to the standard of living a fuller life in which they may hold rewarding jobs and enjoy the fruits of their labor.

Images of Good Schools

When we reflect upon teaching-learning occasions of which we have been a part, invariably such memories are situated. Some image of a place seems to be involved in recalling the experience. The school is typically the site that forms an image for the occasion, while the transaction is viewed in positive or negative ways relative to the impact and importance of the teaching-learning exercised there.

Leadership, too, occurs within spaces. Educational leadership is most often specific to educational sites like classrooms and laboratories. Educators exercising educational leadership are thus affected by both the logic and language of leading and the site-specific nature of the leadership occasions. We recount the leaderlike acts in terms of text while relying upon a subtheme of image. Talk and image become linked in memory.

The good-making or bad-making characteristics of leadership transactions may be moral and ethical in nature. Where we attribute good or bad to the leading, we engage in assignment behavior that colors the exchange and results in our valuing or not valuing the transaction. Yet, the space and place wherein the moral and ethical leadership takes place also affects the decision to regard the act as right or wrong, good or bad. Context is important, whether it be a culture or society, club or clique. The environment conceived of as a place dedicates certain defining characteristics to the quality of the interchange aimed at moving a child, class, or entire school toward some goal.

The notion that the upshot of any leadership transaction ought to be good has a fundamental meaning for the changed shape of the setting. The effort to make educational leadership more ethical has attached to it a kind of context (space and place) that lends itself to that approbation. We are, in the last analysis, left with a change in our text and our context, if all goes the way we wish.

Yet most of the research and writing on educational leadership, ethics and good schools misses the image side of the matter. We are left to feel our way blindly toward the "good school." This book is an effort to lift the scales from our eyes and so lead us to understanding the good school as a place and not merely a concept.

Conclusion

This chapter has sought to demonstrate that a standards-based reform is seeking to transform educational administration into educational leadership. Ethics is incorporated into the ISLLC standards and also many of the state versions of these standards. Knowing and understanding ethical dilemmas is vital to being an ethical leader. The leader should also have certain attitudes and dispositions toward people and judgment. The ethical school leader ought to have the skills to analyze a moral and ethical problem and to bring about a resolution of that dilemma. Ethical leaders cannot blindly follow standards. Thought and creativity are necessary to interpret these benchmarks in terms of changing situations and individuals. Tests of performance need to be seen as less representative of leadership skill than predictive of how leaders will act in future situations. A fully articulated ethics of leadership presents intriguing possibilities for redesigning schools, and ourselves in the process. Beneath any standards-based practice is the need to challenge and rethink the standards and their bearings upon our professional practice. In chapter 3 we shall examine the sources of ethical leadership.

3

The Ethical Leader

"Leadership is a combination of strategy and character. If you must be without one, be without the strategy."
— General H. Norman Schwarzkopf

Ethical leadership may be exercised by principals, teachers, students, or staff. The school, to be a fully moral and ethical space, requires a shared sense of doing what is right and good. The combined decisions of day-to-day leadership aid in building a sense that the school is a moral space, that it is a "good school," while decision-making exercises help strengthen each individual member's moral character.

Issues and dilemmas that call for ethical decision making touch everyone in the school. Failing to prepare all members of the school community to deal with issues of ethics does not indicate that these issues lack importance but that the fracturing and chaotic conditions have invaded the school space and many people are not ready to deal with moral and ethical issues in education. Learning to become more moral and ethical in this environment is possible.

Our schools are becoming increasingly diverse in ethnic, racial, and religious makeup. Sexual orientations, gangs and cliques, and a host of alternative fashions and styles evidenced by tattoos, colors, and body piercings have emerged in the classroom. This diversity and complexity adds to the confusion surrounding everyday value decisions that the principals, teachers, students, and staff need to make. The leader's readiness, no matter what his or her role, to deal with such complexity in a just, wise, and compassionate manner is essential if the school is to succeed.

Three Approaches to Ethics and Educational Leadership

Educational administration experts disagree about the role of ethics in school leadership. A competition, often subtle but nonetheless real, exists among published visions of leadership ethics. Three approaches are evident: ethics for leadership, ethics in leadership, and ethics of leadership.

Ethics for Educational Leadership

One approach is to take historical ethical theories and simply graft them onto school leadership (often idealized). It is assumed that all that is needed to make leadership more moral and ethical is to teach administrators-to-be lessons drawn from the works of Aristotle or the McGuffey Readers (Finn, 1991; Bennett, 1989). If we scratch the surface of this approach, we find a single-minded dedication to a set of classic philosophical principles. We may term this approach perennial, because it continues to apply to every historical period. These theories are easily specified and often operate within a set of rules or standards of ethical practice. It is assumed that if an educational leader adopts this kit bag of old saws, she or he will operate effectively in any moral and ethical crisis.

Ethics in Educational Leadership

A second group of experts, enamored with scientific administration, sees the solution to how schools ought to adopt leadership ethics in a researched approach to "ethics in educational leadership." It is taken for granted that leadership ethics may be discovered only through the methods of scientific research. Once accumulated, data will form a "knowledge base" of school leadership practice. Good schools will result by merely applying these facts to reform. Called a normative approach, this tack assumes that descriptions of organizational leadership characteristics will also serve as recommendations for how we ought to lead schools in the future.

Current best practices of ethical administration stand in for future recommendations as to how leaders ought to act to be ethical. The assumption is a logical one, in that ethics may be studied scientifically, theories specified, and schools changed, in much the way we build a space shuttle. Ignoring culture and individual dynamics, this ethics in education approach is always out of date.

Ethics of Educational Leadership

The third approach to leadership, ethics, and good schools proposes an "ethics of educational leadership." In this approach ethics is seen to be an integral part of leading. Such leadership is always contextual (Duke, 1998). A high regard is placed on a concept of leadership underwritten by a sense that school is a space and has a mission. Leading never takes place in a vacuum. It follows that we should neither import completely a historic (and remote) ethics from outside the cultural context of schooling, nor should we seek our ethics, as Duke (1998) would recommend, in the study of "the immediate context" in which leadership is found.

School issues calling for ethical leadership are easy to detect: Questions of justice and equity, freedom and authority, honesty and integrity, and so forth form the template upon which the ethics of leading must be played out. To that extent every ethical instance of leadership in an organization is normative (recommendational). However, beyond this, we must ask how leadership is to operate such that it recognizes multicultural contexts of organizations, understands competing points of view, and locates practical means for the resolution of moral and ethical conflicts where diversity is prized (Maxcy, 1998).

Certainly, ethics and leadership are related in many ways. Of these three approaches, it is important to see that an ethics *of* educational leadership is superior. Whether practiced by school principals, teachers, students, or staff members, ethics is a part of leadership and not grafted upon it from the outside or added simply for the sake of accomplishing some goal.

Basis for Making a Moral and Ethical Decision

Educators may get most of their ethics from three sources: human nature, individual experience, and the culture at large. Each of these sources, by informing us how we make our moral and ethical decisions, leads to the formation of character.

Human Nature

Since at least the fifth century B.C., philosophers have believed that ethics is a fundamental characteristic attached to our being human. Dogs and cats are not ethical or unethical. Only people seem to have the capacity to think reflectively about how their choices comply with rules or affect other people and nature. The Bible's creation story tells us that because they ate the fruit of the tree of the knowledge of good and evil, Adam and Eve were forced from the Garden of Eden. Knowing about morality is decidedly human in nature.

Yet most of the philosophers who argued that ethics is within our nature as human beings, differed in what they believed human nature to be. Some argued that it was in our human nature to be evil (Thomas Hobbes); others stressed that humans are by nature good (Jean-Jacques Rousseau).

For some theorists, it was natural for humans to seek money, fame, or longevity. Other thinkers spoke of the predilection to join groups and communities. There was a long list of what human beings "naturally" are destined to seek or do. The difficulty with theories of human nature is that they all, by and large, presume that human nature is fixed—that is, the traits found in humans (whatever they may be) are there in everyone and cannot be avoided.

Human nature is not like bird nature. It is true that birds build nests from instinct, but do humans have nest-building instincts? Whatever natural instincts we may have had as humans have long been modified by civilization. Yet we find people using the instinct argument to justify moral and ethical choices. For example, on the grounds that it is instinctual for humans to protect themselves, the gun lobby sways legislators to pass new laws protecting the right to bear arms. It is ethical to use guns, because it is in our human nature to protect ourselves and our families.

These kinds of argument from human nature are powerful, yet equally compelling arguments may be set out against them. It may be claimed that it is in our nature to be competitive. "Survival of the fittest" is our natural tendency, but cooperation is evident as well. Ought this to warrant us having an instinct to join a college fraternity or the Audubon Society?

Personal Experience

Certainly one of the forces of the past half century has been the search for the self. As Christopher Lasch pointed out in his book The Minimal Self (1984), self-realization remains the most worthwhile desire for most Americans. We have but to look at all the self-help and pop psychology books on the bookstore shelves to note the consequence of our increased affluence has been a near obsession with ourselves.

It is not uncommon for personal advancement to come into conflict with communal goals. Writing in 1950, John L. Childs noted the change:

Our schools have long been torn between two moralities—the morality of individual success as measured by pecuniary gain in the private competitive system, and the morality of individual success as measured by socially useful work consciously directed to the welfare of the whole community. It is time education made up its mind as to the kind of America it wants, and sought to educate the young on the basis of that integrated morality. . . ." (236)

In the last fifty years, the close face-to-face communities of the agrarian past have been displaced by giant corporations with corporate philosophies and corporate morals. In the face of this overwhelming organization of human productivity, individuals have been driven to try to preserve their minimal self (Lasch, 1984).

When we view the schools as spacial organizations, it is possible to see this same impulse affecting school goals and decisions. Individuals— educators, parents, students, and school staff—feel at the mercy of what the school organization may value. Efficiency, productivity, and large-scale mass instruction replace the individual attention and personal caring desired by individuals (Noddings, 1984). As a backlash to this lack of personal say-so in the moral and ethical direction of organizations, James Q. Wilson (1993) argues that each person is his own moral compass, possessing a "moral sense" of right and wrong. Individuals have a responsibility to exercise the moral sentiments of sympathy, fairness, self-control, and so forth, and we all know what the right and virtuous are, if we but pay attention to our conscience.

Culture

Of all of the sources of ethics, the organizational culture of schooling, from preschool to university, is marked by disagreement as to what "good" in general, and "good school" in particular, may mean. While personal experience issues may cause confusion and illogic relative to leadership in the search for good living, any worthwhile moral and ethical leadership philosophy ought to identify culture with the individual's vision of the good—the good life, the good organization, and so on.

One of the potential points where educators gain an understanding of how morals and ethics interact with educational organizations is in professional preparation programs. Typically, future school administrators are exposed to a curriculum and texts aimed at making them credentialed principals or superintendents of schools. Too often these formal training sessions are sorely lacking in moral and ethical philosophy (Strike & Ternasky, 1993). At best, leaders-to-be may have a single course or section of a course that deals with ethics and administration or management. Ethics, if treated at all in their mainstream educational administration textbooks, is relegated to a few pages or a chapter. "Professional readings" texts, supplemental to the hard-core school administration best-sellers, are not much better, for they may treat ethics or leadership, but rarely both. Yet these paltry cultural value sources are critical to our school-based moral and ethical decision making (Bull, Fruehling & Chattergy, 1992).

Little effort is made, where leadership ethics and school reform are dealt with seriously, to focus upon recent dynamic transformations in the cultures of advanced nations and the demands such changes make upon our theoretical and practical grasp of the changed moral and ethical character of schools. Entire genres of educational administration research and writing have overlooked these culture shifts, in the vain hope that old-fashioned ways of thinking and writing about values and education will continue to serve us. Increasingly it is evident that such standard moral and ethical training fare will not do; educators, school board members, parents, and, increasingly, students recognize these as outdated prescriptions, and we see that educational administration experts are simply "preaching to their own choirs."

Within the social sciences, a study of the deep and subtle layers of an emerging cultural change pits advocates of this old-fashioned modernism against a newer postmodernism (Rosenau, 1992). As this debate filters down to controversies surrounding school reform, dialogues reveal new efforts are under way to reconceptualize schools; to understand and respecify the interplay between moral and ethical theory and practice; and to test the practical outcomes as these confront school reform proposals (English, 1994; Maxcy, 1995).

Except for a brief period prior to World War II, educational administration scholars in the twentieth century have always striven to make school keeping into "a science of management," with a variety of sociologies and psychologies attached to it (Callahan, 1961; Foster, 1986; English, 1992). Unfortunately, the moral and ethical dimension dropped out quite early, so that by the 1990s ethical administration had become an oxymoron (Murry, 1995; McKerrow, 1997).

Today, moral and ethical recommendations for improved school governance tend to be general in nature and only applicable to abstract practice (Beyer, 1997). Set in linguistic form and relying upon mathematical-logical moves, academic conceptions of moral and ethical problems and solutions celebrate plural theory-based interpretations, easily defer to quasi legal codes of conduct, or simply appeal to the passion to care for and nurture others. Meanwhile, the objects of uplift—students and teachers—gather their models of morality and ethics from TV and films. Enchanted by soap operas and blockbuster movies, and more recently the Internet, power and control blur the distinction between compassionate caring and sexual harassment, date rape and courtship, academic dishonesty and "getting ahead." Images of morality are increasingly drawn from "life on the screen," rather than from reading Aristotle or Kant (Turkle, 1995).

Theories of Ethics

Over the centuries, philosophers have formed or ascribed to certain theories of ethics. These theories help us identify the key arguments and types of decisions we make when we engage in ordinary moral and ethical judgments. While these schools of thought are of interest, they often fail to appear in any formally precise way in our moral and ethical choices. Suffice it to say that theories of ethics instruct us to take greater pains with our choices and to pay attention to the reasons for our choices and likely criticisms of our thinking.

Traditionalism

By all measures, traditionalism as a moral and ethical approach has had the longest and most popular run in human history. Begun in the medieval era (1000–1500) and flourishing in sixteenth-century Britain, it came to America when the Pilgrims landed on the shores of New England in the early 1600s. Building upon an interpretation of religious writings, traditionalists believed that humans are evil by nature, fallen creatures who are born in sin.

From an ethical and educational perspective, parents were expected to teach their children to know right from wrong. Knowing how to read meant that children could understand when the devil was tricking them into doing sinful things. Traditionalism was composed of a set of moral and ethical rules, drawn in part from the Bible but also distilled from the experiences of a segregated and abused religious sect that sought to build a holy community, or "City Upon a Hill," as a beacon to reflect God's desires for humanity.

Traditionalism relies upon the methods of authority, revelation, and intuition to warrant its rules and maxims. You should know that it is best to do X or Y or Z because you were taught this! You have read this ethical ideal in the scriptures, Communist Manifesto, Mao's "Little Red Book," or elsewhere, and therefore you must follow it. Or, you "know it in your heart" that this dietary rule or dress code is proper to follow. Never are such rules negotiable or interpreted for a cultural or social circumstance. The rules are fixed for all time. It is our duty to follow the letter of the law.

Traditionalism in ethics is alive and well today. When we read in the newspapers that parents are lobbying their public school board members to allow prayers before football games or during school hours, or when we hear that someone has demanded the librarian remove a book from the school library because it has "offensive language" in it, we are witnessing traditionalists in operation. It is presupposed that the rules are absolutely right and everyone ought to know this and follow them. Yet, the "rules" may be those of born-again Christians, Muslims, Mormons, Roman Catholics, or many others. The mistake is to believe that your faith and rules are the only ones and must be adhered to by everyone else.

Realism

The realist tradition in ethics and education is really a number of approaches with similar characteristics. Realism is classical in the sense that it is found in the writings of ancient Greek philosophers. During the Middle Ages, realism was popularized by Scholastics and neo-Thomists. Today, the educational philosophy referred to as perennialism is a version of realism.

One fundamental feature ties all realists together: the belief that certain ideas never die, but rather are perennially useful solutions to recurring social dilemmas. Beginning with Aristotle (384–322 B.C.), realists were convinced that people ought to strive to do what is ethical. The good man and the good state went hand in hand. We may learn how to become good from study and we can achieve this knowledge through experience. Art (sculpture, music, etc.) helps in showing people how to be ethical as it teaches us balance and harmony, essential to leading a moderated life.

During modern times, Michel de Montaigne (1533–1592) and John Milton (1600–1674) were realists. And in the twentieth century, Mortimer Adler and Robert Maynard Hutchins were realists. It is Adler and Hutchins who had the most impact on education in recent times. Adler as a professor of philosophy and Hutchins as the president of the University of Chicago created the Great Books program and published the Great Books.

Ethics, it was believed by the realist, is learned and practiced in terms of certain truths about the world, moral thinking, and human nature. These truths guide us, if we study them properly, to make moral and ethical decisions no matter if we are ancient Greeks or modern Americans. By reading the "Great Ideas" we learn that we must be ethical to be good citizens. We learn that each moral and ethical crisis we face has been faced before and there is a well-thought-out textbook answer to it. Study and discussion are the only means to becoming an ethical leader.

Utilitarianism

One of the most popular forms of consequentialism, utilitarianism owes its origins to Jeremy Bentham and John Stuart Mill. These British philosophers held that the most important consideration in any moral and ethical decision is the impact it has on others. Happiness was deemed the good toward which human beings naturally strive. "The greatest good for the greatest number" became the maxim of utilitarians who sought to influence society.

Subjectivism

The subjectivist believes that there are no moral and ethical "facts" and no one is "right" when it comes to moral and ethical choices. If we say "stealing is wrong," we are just expressing our subjective judgment. No scientific methods or social science expertise can tell us anything about correct moral and ethical choices. No one's moral or ethical opinion is any better than anyone else's.

Existentialism

Existentialism is an offshoot of subjectivism. It had its origins in the French Revolution (1789–1799) but is most often connected to French philosopher Jean-Paul Sartre (1905–1980). The existentialists saw no ultimate meaning or purpose in human existence. Without authority from outside, we are left with the belief that we are fully responsible for every choice we make. When we are totally free, the prospect of making a moral and ethical decision becomes enormous. Centering upon the self, Sartre believed that we are abandoned or alone in the universe. He argued that one of the dangers we as individuals face is living our lives in "bad faith." People who act as if they are happy or pretend that they are doing what is good or right are acting in bad faith, he reasoned. To be authentic in your moral and ethical choices, you must be serious about choosing, take responsibility for your choices, and recognize that there is no God or Nature to bail us out.

Emotivism

Charles L. Stevenson, an American philosopher, made improvements on subjectivism, or the belief that all ethical or moral statements are an expression of an individual's personal beliefs. For Stevenson, ethical and moral claims are merely expressions of our emotions. Language is used in many ways, one of which is to express our attitude toward something. If a teacher says, "I believe abortion is immoral," she is not expressing a fact, but rather her feelings. Such expressions of emotion cannot be right or wrong. Thus, morals and ethics are not about knowledge or facts; quite the contrary, they are about our psychological dispositions and expressed feelings.

Naturalism

The most popular theory of ethics today is ethical naturalism. Owing to John Dewey, naturalism was introduced to philosophy of education and has had a wide impact. By naturalism we mean the philosophy that asserts that moral and ethical dilemmas may be investigated using human intelligence and particularly the tools of social science. Decisions as to what to do in such dilemmas may be assessed as right or wrong, or good or bad based upon inquiry into the "natural world" of social relations (Pidgen, 1991).

Naturalists are somewhat like realists in their belief that moral judgments may be known and thus detected as true or false. However, they differ in their belief that the facts of ethics change with time and conditions. By placing morals and ethics under the lens of inquiry, naturalists part company with emotivists who claim we are just expressing an irrational feeling, and intuitionists, who believe that good is an unanalyzable property of things that we know when we see it. While naturalists situate individual human choosers in the moral and ethical equation, they do not release them from authority. That authority is human intelligence and the tools of investigation, not abandonment or isolation. (Naturalists are in sync with today's focus on public morality and less concerned about traditionalists' and existentialists' private moral or ethical worries.)

Two Dispositions: Human Rights and the Common Good

Two moral dispositions or attitudes stand out, as Fukuyama tells us in his book *Trust* (1995): the morality that honors individual success, and the attitude that favors a kind of collective or common good of the entire institution, community, state, or nation. Since the 1960s, the force pushing for our consideration of individuals and their rights has met head-on with the other, more historical force, which is struggling to get us to preserve and advance the common good. Ethics of educational leadership must keep an eye on both moral and ethical dispositions, balancing the rights of individuals with the good of the entire school.

Rights

Kristja Falvo, mother of three pupils, Elizabeth, Philip, and Erica, sued the Owasso, Oklahoma, school district. She argued that the teacher's time-saving practice (used across the country) of relying on students to grade other students' homework and quizzes was wrong. Mrs. Falvo sued the school on two grounds: (1) that the school system violated her children's constitutional right to privacy under the Fourteenth Amendment; and (2) that the school system violated the children's legal rights under the Family Educational Rights and Privacy Act of 1974.

Some teachers in the Owasso school district teach large classes of as many as 140 pupils in presecondary schools. To save time, these teachers allow pupils to grade the homework of fellow students. Once the correct and incorrect answers are marked on the papers, they are returned to their owner. These scores may be reported by students orally in class or reported in private to the teacher. The scores may or may not be recorded in the teacher's grade book.

In October 2000 a three-judge panel of the U.S. Court of Appeals for the Tenth Circuit threw out the charge that this grading practice was unconstitutional, but it upheld Falvo's complaint under FERPA. The court further pointed out that an "educational record" is defined as those records, files, documents, and other materials that (1) contain information directly related to a student and (2) are maintained by an educational agency or institution or by a person acting for such an agency or institution. Homework and quizzes are "education records," one judge declared, and therefore must be kept in confidence (private). The Owasso attorney appealed the finding to the Supreme Court. The issue seemed to center on the difference in belief about the meaning of privacy in elementary and middle schools.

Under a finding that this grading practice violates the children's right to privacy, educators would tend to assign less homework and give fewer pop quizzes, Jerry A. Richardson, the Owasso attorney, argued. In the name of protecting the pupil's right to keep his or her scores and grades private, the public schools of this country, he argued, must then grant a hearing to every parent seeking to challenge the correctness of any grade recorded in a teacher's grade book. This practice would "play havoc" with even the most mundane tasks teachers engage in day to day, the Owasso attorney claimed.

If the Supreme Court does not overturn the Tenth Circuit Court, the law will hold school districts to the rule that they cannot allow students to grade one another's identifiable homework or test paper. Nor can teachers require students to call out their own grades in class for recording by the teacher. Both of these instructional acts would violate a student's rights (unless the student's parent has specifically consented to this practice).

Regardless of what the Supreme Court rules, national attention to this case has alerted school leaders that they should move more aggressively to protect student rights in the sensitive area of evaluation. Implicit in this problem of testing is the issue of public versus private grading practices. School leaders should tell teachers and teacher aides that they should review their use of grading practices that compromise a student's privacy. One student probably ought not to correct another identifiable student's homework, quizzes, or tests. Calling out his or her grade on any assignment in class should be discouraged.

These reactionary practices are informed not so much by the letter of the law but by a new sensitivity to areas that the legal arm of the nation has moved to cover. As an ethical leader, sensitivity to such border cases (legal cases under contest) requires you to keep an ethical and moral eye on the harm or potential harm school practices may have for all concerned. This sensitivity may never appear in a code of teacher or administrator ethics. Nonetheless, ethics covers more ground than law, and ethical concerns often predate legislation and legal decisions.

Finally, it is vital for the ethical leader to know the various laws and policies affecting the rights of students and teachers. The Family Educational Rights and Privacy Act (FERPA) mandates that school authorities not divulge student records. Any school that reports the grades of a student to the media would be breaking the law. Such facts are not to be made public. Educational leaders must respect the privacy of students in this arena.

Such clear-cut legal pronouncements are narrower than the larger concern that educators not violate privacy rights of students, teachers, or staff. Where the law does not cover a particular instance, there may still be a moral and ethical problem with revealing matters that are to be held in confidence.

The Common Good

We can thank the Enlightenment philosophers and our own Founding Fathers for introducing us to the concept of the common good. What thinkers like Jean-Jacques Rousseau, Thomas Jefferson, and Benjamin Franklin had in mind when they addressed the nature of the state was that a political entity may be made up of many states and individuals, each with their own desires, interests, and will to succeed. The thirteen "united" states each had to be convinced to curb some of their own desires, interests, and needs so that the good of the entire nation could be maintained.

Schools are not different from nations in this respect. Somehow the good of the school must be considered versus the good of individuals making claims upon the resources and skills the school offers. There is only so much money, talent, knowledge, and space to go around.

Part of what it means to be engaged in an ethical leadership approach to management, administration, stewardship, piloting, and so on is to look carefully at the good of the school as a whole and to balance this with the individual's rights within the school. We ought to secure bonds of social trust, or accept the belief that our transactions as members of the school are tied to the best interests of the entire school and community.

Least Harm

Another disposition is least harm. Some philosophers, like Richard Rorty, argue that the premier disposition we ought to carry into our decisions is to "do the least harm." By seeking not to do damage, and relying upon "social hope," Rorty (1999) anticipates that the good of the individual as well as of the society may be realized. Critics point out that this faint-hearted effort to be virtuous does not add much to our lives or institutions. In Rorty's defense, he may be more interested in avoiding the bad policies of eager-beaver leaders who are mindless and witless.

The Good School

If contemporary school reforms are something of a spectacle, it is the kind of spectacle that reoccurs. Today's school choice advocates sound like Horace Mann pumping for free, tax-supported schools in early nineteenth century Massachusetts. The essential details may differ, but the moralistic language and moral realism remain. School reform has become high theater, with superintendents and school boards fighting it out on cable TV. So image-driven is this spectacle that we cannot locate answers or redemption in the techno-scientific language of standard educational research reports. The words fail to capture the color and dynamics of the scene. The result is that parents and school reform followers are lulled into assuming that what is said is what is seen. The idea of the good school is cloaked in a variety of proposals for school reform that seem to pivot on conceptions of the institutional good, where *institution* is equated with *school*, and *good* is equated with *effective, productive, achievement-oriented*, and so forth. (Finn, 1991).

However, in the past was a good school rarely seen as a moral or ethical school. This tendency to identify good with productive value, and moral and ethical with humanistic value has been corrected by some recent researchers in educational administration (Jackson et al., 1993; Murry, 1995; Roy, 1996). Jackson and colleagues demonstrated that morals and ethics were overt as well as subtle and pervasive aspects of classrooms. Murry's (1995) research found that being a moral leader in an urban school translates into a number of different strategies. Roy (1996) discovered that the "moral elementary school" is both explicitly moral and implicitly moral. Her study of principals focused on their disciplinary acts as moral expressions of their values, but they also communicated moral and ethical values in a myriad of actions such as greeting students, praising teachers in their work, speaking with parents, and arranging the furniture and pictures in the central office to offer a more welcoming image. In these studies, the good school comes into view as a unique kind of community in which individuals are bonded by moral and ethical values.

The Principal and Ethical Leadership

The school administrator holds a position in the school in addition to exercising certain power. In this post it is possible to exceed the requirements of the task and exact a toll on teachers, counselors, staff members, and students. Excessive use of authority can do harm.

One problem area of increasing seriousness is that of harassment. Simply put, harassment is exercising power or force over another to secure one's own desires. The most common form of harassment is bullying. The use of power to get one's way through threats or actual acts of force is unethical because it disregards the other person's interests. As Kant would say, it treats other persons as a means to your own ends, and not as an end in themselves. We must consider that a person has certain dignities that come with the territory. Cultural history and conventions of law have established a line between what is in one person's interest and not in another's. Freedom to think and act in certain ways is no guarantee that thoughts and actions may be used to enslave, dominate, intimidate, or in other ways threaten another person.

Sexual harassment involves acts against another human being in the interest of satisfying one's own sexual appetite. Forcing a subordinate to exchange sex for promotion, sex for salary increases, or sex for any facet of the job is a gross misappropriation of that person's freedom and dignity. Unfortunately, sexual harassment in a variety of guises is common in schools and colleges where department heads, deans, and other college officials have been accused of (and disciplined for) harassing subordinates.

The most important thing to consider in making practical decisions about harassment is to see harassing acts as exercises in power. As in rape, which is not a crime of passion but one of power, the victim is stripped of dignity by the attacker. A difference in the harassment cases is that often the victims must be quiet and suffer repeatedly attacks because the system rewards the criminal and discourages the victim. Until schools and colleges begin to punish harassing attacks on teachers and faculty by administrators, we will have a system in which morale is lowered and personal esteem attacked by the powerful.

No argument for institutional effectiveness as a function of harassing and intimidating administration will wash. The costs of harassment are high and no institution escapes negative press from allowing such behavior to continue. After all, who wishes to work in a school where the goals of the organization are considered more important than the rights of the employee?

The Ethical Teacher-Leader

While the school principal may make many moral and ethical decisions in a day's time, the teacher seems to have the enviable opportunity to locate moral and ethical problems in students' lives and help correct them. Teachers use moral and ethical strategies and maintain attitudes favoring individual rights and the common good of the school when they deal with students. At times they look to the standard or rule and what it would mean if they did not honor it in a case. At other times they may consider the consequences of their decision for a particular student, thus electing not to follow the letter of the rule. This is what makes ethics so important. There is no clear-cut guide to making decisions of a moral and ethical nature.

Teachers and Students: Relationships

Not too long ago, the newspapers and television were filled with stories of a female teacher who had sex with a male student and gave birth to a child. The teacher was tried for this crime but became pregnant again by the same student. She claimed they were in love. The boy was too young to assume parenting responsibilities. The result was that the former teacher was jailed and the children put in foster care.

In another case, a predatory student sought out his female teacher and aggressively sought a relationship. The female teacher's will was broken down and she consented to the relationship. The teacher was deemed at fault even though the student had initiated the entire affair.

Teacher-student relationships of a close and personal kind are not unknown in history. The most famous case took place in the twentieth century. A beautiful young female student, Heloise, had an affair with her tutor, the great philosopher Peter Abelard. In his Scito Teipsum (Know Thyself), Abelard wrote that ethics was not observing events and judging them in terms of rules, but rather listening to one's heart. It was possible to say that one who had good intentions was not unethical. Heloise's uncle did not subscribe to this philosophy, and when he heard of Abelard's behavior with his niece, he had his revenge. The consequence was that Heloise was shipped off to a nunnery and Abelard moved to a monastery. When Abelard died after a successful career as a teacher, he was buried with Heloise, thus satisfying a revenge of his own.

In frontier America, Australia, and Canada, it was not uncommon for the students to be older than their teachers. This led to numerous liaisons and marriages. The situation was exacerbated by the fact that by law, female teachers could not be married. Young, unmarried women were often victims of circumstances.

Male teachers seemed to have fared better. Older and more mature than their students, they might date and marry a female student with the blessing of the family and the community. Male teachers could be married or not and still hold their jobs. In addition, male and female teachers tended to move from school to school in search of better teaching conditions and higher pay.

The practice of "boarding around" with the families of students no doubt lent much to the promise of marriage.

Teachers who seek out relationships with their students must be aware of the law against such actions today as well as the moral and ethical repercussions of these relationships. Teachers have a particular trust that they must respect. Students are placed in a teacher's care with the expectation that the student will be taught. Because teaching is sometimes characterized as "a loving relationship" between teacher and student in which the teacher nurtures the senses of the immature learner, we have the potential for difficulties.

Teachers and Educational Research

In this era of accountability and measurement, teachers are being encouraged to do research into educational questions. They may wish to find out which strategies of teaching work best, what discipline procedures produce the most effective outcomes, and so forth.

Should teacher-researchers expose their pupils as human subjects to experiments or other kinds of treatments, or substances that may be potentially harmful? If a teacher wishes to test a new teaching strategy that has a reputation for excellence, is it right for her to teach one class using the strategy and withhold it from a second class she teaches? Is it permissible for a teacher acting as a researcher to lie to students in an experiment he conducts? Is it right for the teacher-researcher to plant actors in social experiments to lead people into doing or saying things they might not otherwise do or say? Should a teacher-researcher take credit for research work he never did? If a researcher takes part in a study, where should his name go on the published report of this work?

One of the newest areas of social science research is research conducted by teachers in their own elementary, middle, and secondary schools (Lagemann, 2000). Often termed practitioner research, or action research, it finds the teachers investigating the classrooms in which they themselves teach (Zeni, 2001). As such, teacher research is less objective than social science research conducted by outsiders (such as university professors, state department of education workers, or paid consultants). Teachers must continue to be associated with colleagues and students well after the research study is conducted. This immersion of the researcher in the school culture affects all those involved in the studies.

In many ways, the teacher-researcher is more likely to select small group experiments for investigations. Thus, teacher-researchers are now more prone to ethical mistakes than a visiting professor might be. They are rarely trained in ethics and typically have fewer research courses at the university. Their inquiries may well fall outside the bounds of watchdog committees as well. The universities have no control over teacher investigations, except insofar as they may be part of university course assignments or class requirements.

No doubt we are in for a new round of mistreatments of human subjects. Students, immature and uninformed about their rights and subject to the teacher on a daily basis, may well be victimized by unethical treatment. Overzealous teacher-researchers may wish to produce data and interpretations quickly (within a semester, let us say). Teacher-researchers may have no professional association or group to turn to for information about the limits their research must respect.

Research by educators falls prey to a number of ethical difficulties. Most often researchers and research activities are charged with deception, a kind word for lying. Infractions have been most numerous as researchers have dealt with human subjects in deceptive ways. Data, knowledge, reports, and evaluations all have suffered from researcher deception. Researchers have been known to manipulate data to bring about a particular outcome they favor. The knowledge purportedly derived from research designs and methods has been intentionally skewed and findings distorted. In some cases the evaluations and reports are written with the contractor's bias in mind, so that objective reporting is impossible. Another kind of research deception finds researchers lying to subjects in experiments.

The Milgram Experiments

In 1963, Stanley Milgram of Yale University recruited students as subjects in an experiment. They were told they were to be "teachers" and would administer a painful electric shock to "learners" who made mistakes. Milgram did not tell these teachers that the learners were really paid actors and the electric shocks were bogus. The actors were placed in a separate room that could be viewed through a glass window and were wired up to a machine. As this experiment proceeded the actors made more and more mistakes. Milgram and his associates encouraged the teachers to administer higher and higher doses of shock to the learners when they failed. The actors would scream louder and louder as the voltage rose. What Milgram discovered was that the teachers became uneasy and then upset as the voltage they purportedly administered rose. As the screams of agony from the actors increased, the teachers protested that they did not wish to continue and that the subjects were in pain. Nevertheless, 62 percent of the teachers obeyed the experimenters' commands to administer maximum shock. The human subjects ("teachers") had been fooled into revealing a side of their nature that they would never have revealed voluntarily.

Even though the student subjects later learned that they had been manipulated and that the "learners" were really actors, it did not seem to offset the harm done to them when they saw how easily they had capitulated to the experimenters' harsh instructions. As a result of the Milgram studies, psychological experimentation came under strong scrutiny. Such experiments are no longer performed (legally) and the American Psychological Association has adopted a code of ethics that calls for subjects in experiments to give their informed consent to play a part in such testing. Universities, from which most of the social science research emanates, have put into place policies and committees dealing with the humane use of human subjects in research studies. Subjects must give their consent to being used in experiments and all matters affecting them must be set out in advance or the experiments cannot be conducted.

One of the results of such watchdog strategies has been to curb the use of deception in certain kinds of experiments. Another result has been the creation of new ways to gather data without directly interacting with human subjects. Researchers have gravitated to more remote statistical methods and the intervariabilities of the data derived by others. Educational researchers today are less likely to do experimental research, owing to the legal and ethical pitfalls attached to this form of inquiry.

The Ethical Student

A thirteen-year-old Florida student, upset on the last day of classes at the end of the school year because a teacher would not allow him into his classroom to say goodbye to two girls, returned with a gun and shot Mr. Barry Grunow between the eyes. Tried in court as an adult, young Nathaniel Brazill spoke at his sentencing: "Words cannot really express how sorry I am, but they're all I have. . . . As I look back on that day I wish it had not happened and that I could bring Mr. Grunow back. . . . Regardless of what anyone thinks, I never intended to harm Mr. Grunow." (Canedy, 2001). Was Nathaniel a cold-blooded killer or a troubled teenager? In interviews, Nathaniel posed a parallel situation that seemed to warrant his using a gun to kill Mr. Grunow.

He argued that if someone had a million dollars and another person came in with a gun, would not the first person give him the money?

The logic expressed in Nathaniel's remarks reveals a youngster who did not know right from wrong. He justified his bringing a gun to school and using it to threaten and kill a teacher in overly simplistic terms. We may say that he was fixated at the preconventional stage of moral development or Stage I, and in exchange for his selfish interest to speak with two girls, he was willing to kill a teacher. Selfishness is a marked characteristic of the very immature person when it comes to ethics. Here Nathaniel neither felt nor knew the compulsion to treat others fairly or with caring consideration: he was solely driven by his teenage desire to see these young women. In hindsight, Nathaniel's remarks are neither fully contrite (he does not appear to realize the harm done to Grunow and his family), nor does he recognize the fuller consequences of his act. Willing to break a rule and unaware of the results of his act, Nathaniel went ahead and solved his problem with force.

We have seen how our human nature, personal experience, and culture affect our moral and ethical decisions and our capacity to make them.

Discipline

Perhaps the most serious problem facing educators and schoolteachers in particular is discipline. However, the issues attached to discipline are many, and control of the students and classroom often mask the deeper concerns students and teachers may have. Few teachers avoid incidents in their daily work that call for either serious attention or punishment.

- A third grade child fails a test. Squirming in her seat, she draws the teacher's attention. The teacher calls upon her to recite her grade on the exam. The student bolts from the classroom and is caught by the principal running out the front door of the school.
- A freshman male student during physical education class is picked up by a senior "student teaching aide" and dropped on his head in front of the rest of the class. The bully, a member of the football team, criticizes the boy for not trying out for the football team, calling him "yellow belly" and "sissy." Two years later the coach observes the student urinating on several football helmets in the locker room. The student is brought before the principal for disciplining.
- A second grader is spotted by a teacher in the lunchroom showing his fellow classmates a revolver. The teacher disarms the student and marches

him to the principal's office. Because the "no guns on school grounds" law requires calling the police, he is led away by police officers and taken to the station. The principal calls his parents.

• Two female seventh graders fighting in the hallway are observed by a teacher. One of the students strikes the teacher, causing her to fall and hit her head on an open locker door. Bloodied and dazed, the teacher is rescued by another teacher and taken to the hospital, where she is diagnosed with a concussion and receives six stitches on the side of her head. The former beauty queen cries herself to sleep that night and cannot be consoled by her husband.

These cases are typical of the sorts of experiences that occur daily in the schools of our nation. Much worse has happened and will happen in the future.

Plagiarism

While the cases of extreme student violence are rare, cases of plagiarism are more frequent. Plagiarism involves academic dishonesty. When students plagiarize, they copy another person's work either not citing the source of the work or getting permission from the owner of the work. Plagiarism is not just a student problem. With the growth of the Internet, essays, reports, articles, and even entire books may be found on web pages. It is quite easy to slip and copy these creations without acknowledging their source. Increasingly, students do not even realize they are plagiarizing when they do so.

Teachers may help with the problem of plagiarism by telling their classes about academic dishonesty and why it is wrong to copy someone else's work. Sometimes, students are ignorant of the rules against plagiarizing and merely need to be taught that it is wrong. On other occasions, a student may know that it is wrong but not realize that the same rule applies in the context of the Internet. Sources must be cited and direct quotes need to be in quotation marks in the new work.

When a child is aware of the rules, breaks them anyway in a knowing way, and is to be punished, the teacher can use a number of decision-making criteria. If the school has a code of student conduct and a published version is distributed to every student, and if the student knows what plagiarism is, ignorance of the rule cannot be used to waive discipline procedures. When a student is caught plagiarizing, confronted with the evidence, and has no significant defense, the teacher may wish to give the student a failing grade for the assignment, contact the principal or counselor, or send the case forward to a school court (if one exists). To deal with the matter from a justice standpoint means enforcing the rules as they apply to the ethical infraction.

There may be instances where the student requires a simple reprimand. Very young students, those with special needs, pupils with disturbed family backgrounds, and so forth, may call for different treatment. Here justice needs to be tempered with mercy and the caring attitude is required.

Bullying

Increasingly, taking advantage of other children because of their size, weight, sex, or age is being singled out as "bullying" (harassment in the adult world). We know that some children seem to be just naturally more aggressive. Other children come from family or socioeconomic conditions where taking advantage of others is standard fare. Our culture seems to value the strong. Television and films portray the heroes as bigger and stronger than their enemies.

When children engage in bullying, it is important to correct the actions before they get out of hand. Bullying is not random, and it tends to become systematic over time. A child who takes advantage of others (stealing their lunch money or bus fare, for example) should be disciplined. If the infractions continue, parents need to be alerted and called in for a conference.

Children who are bullies can become adults who harass others. The symptoms are often a desire for power and control over other people. Quick justice may be the best alternative, or a caring approach where strict consequences could be harmful to the child. Whatever the course of action, we need to recognize that bullying is morally and ethically wrong and should be curtailed as early as possible.

Staff and Ethical Leadership

A good school requires that all persons involved with the school have a sense of the moral character of the space they occupy. School staff members, such as secretaries, clerks, dieticians, janitors, and bus drivers all have a vested interest in a school that is safe and secure from the threats of lying, cheating, stealing, and other unethical acts.

Keeping to a sound set of ethical standards or principles helps. The secretary who lies on the phone about the whereabouts of the assistant principal is not making the image of the school more honest. The bus driver who drinks on the job and misses drop-offs is not contributing to the vision of the school as a moral and ethical space.

Caring and justice need to be used in day-to-day dealings with others. An ethical leadership manifested by staff members will help raise the moral and ethical level of the school. Accrediting agencies, school boards, state departments of education, and other groups are looking carefully at the moral and ethical atmosphere of the school and how staff members contribute to that atmosphere.

Stealing

One of the problems staff seem to get involved in is stealing. Having access to the supply room or petty cash poses a lure some cannot resist. Taking pens, pads of paper, or money is unethical; stealing from your employer, the school district or university, is wrong. Borrowing these resources is also unethical, because while the items or money are absent, they are not available to the school. Often staff members forget to replace them or lose track of how much they have borrowed. Fines and jail terms may result.

It is important to separate what is yours from what belongs to the school, and to keep this clearly separated at all times.

Favors

Exchanging duties for favors is unethical. It is a trap and a lure to see one's self benefiting from helping others, for example, by special counseling or tracing lost grades. However, expecting a payback for performing one's duties, duties for which the school district or university pays a salary, is wrong. It is a matter of being paid twice for the same act.

Suggestions on How to Improve Ethical Leadership by Principals, Teachers, Students, and Staff

As we have learned, the sources of morals and ethics come to us from our human nature, experience, and the culture we live in. By thinking about and making moral and ethical choices, we develop over time a consistent pattern of choosing. How we approach an ethical dilemma becomes ingrained with practice. This succession of decisions and tracing our decisions to concrete ends leads us to develop moral character. The study of numerous moral values or principles may aid us in building our moral character.

Virtues as Dispositions to Act

In the practical moral and ethical leadership advanced in this book, the conception of virtue is significant. The Greeks and Romans spoke of virtues and listed them separately. Chastity, kindness, honesty, courage, modesty, temperance, toleration, and a number of other concepts were given the title "virtue." Yet these virtues, as Dewey and Tufts (1908) tell us, cannot be defined as separate entities because each so-called virtue expresses an interest in terms of institutions and events that are ever changing. Instead, we need to think of a virtue as a kind of attitude or disposition regarding something we are interested in pursuing.

Recall that the new standards for principals speak of each standard as having a set of dispositions and behaviors that accompany it. Evaluation of principal performance, then, will be judged relative to how well the individual principal understands the standard, is disposed to embrace it in his or her leadership, and actually acts in terms of the standard. We may also argue that the understanding of these dispositions plays a part in the leader's own moral character. The ancient Greeks led us to this conclusion.

We have discussed two virtues, a concern for the rights of individuals and a regard for the common good. The following may be added to this list of leadership virtues.

Courage

Having a courageous attitude is necessary if the principal is to do battle with the forces that would hurt individuals or tear down the school. The war against the negative and counterproductive is constant; laziness and bad habits often provoke the weak to seek the easy way out. The principal needs courage to follow the course.

The opposite of courage is cowardice. A leader who runs away from tough choices is cowardly. The disposition to be bold and hold the line in a tough moral dilemma is an aspect of the leadership character.

Temperance

Temperance here refers to holding one's emotions at bay. While it is intemperate to engage in steamy rhetoric, it is the temperate principal that measures her words and considers their effect.

Intemperate people give in to their desires and emotions. As small children, we naturally do this. When we reach adulthood, it is expected that we have more gravity and refrain from indulging our every whim and wish. Balancing the emotional with the intellectual is important here.

Prudence

To be prudent is to listen carefully before acting. To judge and weigh the outcomes of a decision against the costs of making that choice engages prudence.

An educational leader who repeatedly makes snap decisions is thought to be imprudent. Practical and reflective decision making calls for gathering data and information, weighing this in terms of the options presented, and carefully testing out (hypothetically and in action) the results of the decision.

Honesty

The honest principal is always more effective than one who lies. There should be a rule posted on the schoolroom wall that says "honesty is the best policy." A dishonest leader must be very creative and possess a photographic memory! She must be creative to fashion new excuses in place of the true reasons for things. An almost total recall is necessary to backfill for lies told previously and to set the new lie in with the old ones. Most colleagues know when a school leader is dishonest. Most importantly, students can often sense it.

Will and Performance

The truly ethical leader has not only a knowledge of ethics and the virtues and dispositions to carry out ethical actions, but also the will to use them. William James once wrote that if you wish to jump across a deep crevasse, you need to have faith that you can make the leap before you try it. For if you do not, you will surely find yourself falling into the void.

Acquiring a will to do something is important, particularly for moral and ethical decisions, and requires a desire to expend effort. Such will is clearly the result of practice and habit. The drug addict who wishes to break his addiction needs the will to do so. If he lacks that will, and faith in his success, he is doomed from the start.

So it is for moral and ethical leadership: we must cultivate the proper disposition or virtue, and we must cultivate our will and resolve to put our decision into action. In this way, moral and ethical decisions are practical in quite a new sense. They are practical because they are matters of our private and professional practice.

Working at Becoming an Ethical Leader

Whether for student seeking election to a school office, a teacher joining an important curriculum committee, or a school principal faced with newspaper reporters seeking to learn more about a crime at the school, leadership is fraught with moral and ethical considerations. The conscientious person must exercise reflective skill in making choices and in so doing seek to make them the most informed and most consistent with his or her personal character. The school as a cultural space and social space must be considered, and every decision of a moral kind must be weighed regarding its effect upon the rules and the people. This entire process works to improve the conditions within the school space and it works to improve the moral character of the leader.

Conclusion

In this chapter we have seen that the ethical leader, whether in the role of school administrator, teacher, student, or staff member, ought to seek to create an ethical leadership approach. Two moralities vie for our attention: the morality of individual rights and the morality of the common good. We saw how ethics is strongly linked to leadership and has its source in conceptions of human nature, experience, and culture. We have explored more attitudes or dispositions of a moral and ethical kind—courage, temperance, prudence, and honesty. Finally, we have learned that, rather than a given, ethical leadership is a matter of hard work and consistent development, the product of which is moral character.

4

Becoming an Ethical Educational Leader

"The creative function as a whole is the essence of leadership"
— Chester Barnard, *Functions of the Executive*

Leadership Ethics: Nature or Nurture?

Can leaders be taught to be ethical? Aristotle wrestled with this question, and in some circles it continues to plague us today. On the one hand, it is possible to argue that ethics is biological in nature and mostly a matter of inherited characteristics. On the other hand, other experts claim that ethics is learned from parents and family, peers, church or temple members, and the community at large. Certainly, formal schooling would be one of the most powerful agencies for preparing us for moral and ethical decision making. The truth probably lies between these two extremes of biological inheritance and learned response.

It has often been assumed that an ethical person is someone who has an inherited ability to think and act ethically. The capacity for being thoughtful, caring, just, open, trusting, sensitive, and so forth may be inherited traits we acquire through biological channels. Our choices, and even our choice of life career (teacher, personal trainer, gossip columnist, etc.) may be a result of these genetic traits and personality characteristics. This nature explanation has fueled a number of extreme philosophies, most prominently Social Darwinism. The advocates of inherited moral and ethical character found that it was divided among people based upon their social status. Members of the upper classes, or certain races, were credited with superior moral and ethical capacities. Herbert Spencer, the father of sociology, argued that some people were just naturally superior owing to their fitness for survival. Adolf Hitler believed that the Aryan race and its members were superior in all ways, including the capacity to make moral and ethical decisions, owing to pure bloodlines.   .

These extreme philosophies led to the "genetics movement," a concerted effort by some to control breeding of humans and to seek ways to exterminate members of perceived inferior races and social classes ("the final solution"), was justified by the study of family trees. Sterilization experiments have also been conducted in the United States on individuals with developmental disabilities and diseases. From the 1930s to the early 1970s, the U.S. Public Health Service studied over 400 African-American men in Macon County, Alabama, who had syphilis. These men were neither told that they had contracted the disease nor offered treatment even after the discovery that penicillin made treatment more effective. Social hygiene curriculum materials and courses were circulated throughout the United States supporting the idea of social health through sterilization. At times, the ethical educational leader was pressured to adopt these radical measures or be seen as anti-American.

The Study of Administration

For centuries, moral virtue was tightly connected with leadership. The New Testament and writings of medieval philosophers praised rulers who could put personal desires aside for the good of their people. Niccolo Machiavelli (1469–1527), an Italian politician and political theorist, rejected this tradition. He established the first modern approach to teaching leadership when he published *The Prince* (1512–1513) in an effort to curry favor with men in the government of Florence and thus regain his lost job. While Machiavelli's writing was inflammatory and his statements rash, his purpose was to set out a curriculum and method for teaching the prince how to lead the state. When it came to morals and politics, he preached to the young sovereign that he must do whatever is necessary to preserve the state. While royalty in the past had aimed at being virtuous rulers, Machiavelli taught that they must be ruthless in governing efficiently.

School Administration

Only three nations—the United States, Canada, and Australia—currently underwrite educational administration as a legitimate field of study and provide for licensure or certification of principals, school heads, and other educational officials. Within these nations, programs for the preparation of school administrators vary widely along the line of theory versus practitioner-oriented study. Calls from at least one strong interest group, the UCEA in the United States, propose that preparation of school principals cease being a function of masters-level university work and be shunted up to a doctoral-level program of study.

In the United States, for example, little systematic work is required in ethics and morals. Whereas the preparation of engineering and business management students encompasses courses in ethics that address the unique problems in these two areas, educational administration preparation programs more often than not include no treatment of ethical matters whatsoever.

Therefore the question before us is: How should educational leaders be prepared to deal with the moral/ethical problems they face in their work?

In the vast majority of countries, educational administration is neither an activity separate from teaching nor essential. When we trace the statistics on school effectiveness, nations without an educational administration field seem to do as well as or better than nations that have adopted this model. However, a lack of moral/ethical preparation for school leaders does not seem to excuse us from the responsibility for exercising moral/ethical judgment.

The Moral and Ethical Domain

Increasingly, educators are coming to realize that schooling encompasses more than the simple reproduction of social life. Education involves values—moral and ethical—which emerge from living and require reassessment from time to time. Were we to ask if educational administration is more like geometry or more like poetry, the latter seems to make more sense. In geometry the answer is either correct or incorrect, based on the theorems of geometry. A moral and ethical decision in the school may call upon a number of rules, some of which are contradictory, subject to interpretation, and in other ways more complex than simple mathematics.

School Leaders Prepared

Studies of the day-to-day activities of educational administrators reveal that they have precious little time to reflect. Decisions must be made on the spot in many instances. Moreover, these decisions may well turn into policies that affect the further direction of events. Thus, the decision is practical and on-the-spot. As Simon (1965) points out, most of our choices are bounded by factors that seriously restrict us. Hence, our moral and ethical picks are "satisficing" rather than fully researched and intellectually pondered rational choices. But this feature of choosing does not preclude our selecting the best options given the constraints, and in this sense we may be said to pay more attention to the outcomes than to the boundary conditions. School leaders actively engaged in educational judgments seem to have certain characteristic features:

- Educational judgments of a moral and ethical sort are focused upon educational sources and outcomes (goods).
- Moral and ethical preparation of school principals is facilitated by an intellectual grounding in the domain or territory of school governance.

Moral Character and Leadership

In quite another sense of what it is to possess moral leadership, we find that leaders must possess moral character. It makes little sense to speak of moral leadership if in fact the leader fails to manifest morality in his or her own acts. Further, we see an artificial dichotomy that speaks of moral theory and moral practice. Morality is played out in the day-to-day decisions and consequential behaviors we manifest as humans. Moral talk is simply that—talk. We must, as they say, "put our money where our mouth is."

When we seek to identify these moral character prerequisites for leaders, it is important to regard such ideas as generalized attitudes rather than fixed absolutes. We shall hope that leaders manifest such attitudes most of the time and hold out the option that exceptions follow the rule. In fact, it is perhaps more admirable for leaders to be consistent with regard to their moral principles than so high-minded that they never operationalize any of their platitudes.

Morally invested leadership is built upon the virtue of integrity. In this virtue, we have consistency in one's own private feelings, actions relative to public disposition, and practice. To have integrity, to be integral, seems to be the keystone in operationalized moral leadership. It was integrity that Caesar lacked (or so his opponents tell us), for he was ambitious for himself above Rome. He held his private interests paramount over his publicly held philosophic ends.

To be quixotic, changeable, unpredictable, chaotic in personality—all of these counter the virtue of integrity. A smoothly flowing stream of judgments, an air of predictability, settlement, continuity, and seamless worthwhileness—these attendant qualities frame integrity. Without integrity, the leader degenerates to a less desirable manager of the Simon Legree type.

The moral leader is considered by some to be a mechanical mediator; one who attacks value conflicts and brings about consensus and confluent action. When organizations have goals, and leaders are committed to their realization, moral leaders gather followers and unite them with respect to the ends of the organization. Moreover, it is the duty of the moral leader, as a kind of modern Platonist, to move followers to embrace the higher values over the lower. The moral leader, given this conception, is a kind of ship's captain, navigating rough value waters, galvanizing the crew to action when tides and troughs present danger. Followers are empowered, but only in terms of the administrated objective of reaching some predetermined shore. Charts are studied, positions determined, and a choice finely hewn along vectors studied and preordained. Value choices are engineering picks with costs factored in from the start.

In contrast to this technical view of leaders as moral agents stands the view of moral leadership as a natural part of being a human being. Imprecise and unique decision making, where each choice is likely to shift the meanings of the field of play. This view of moral and ethical problem solving was championed by William James and John Dewey and continues to influence us today under the rubric of "ethical naturalism." The process of becoming moral and ethical is natural, rather than supernatural; it suggests that we grow into moral and ethical persons as we exercise sound thinking and draw upon experience in making our moral and ethical decisions.

Nature and Development as the Source of Ethical Leadership

In the 1960s, psychologists looked at the work of Jean Piaget, a French philosopher and student of child development, for clues as to how adults become moral and ethical. Two researchers, Lawrence Kohlberg and Carol Gilligan, mapped out decidedly different answers to this question.

Lawrence Kohlberg's View of Moral Development

How does a leader grow to become moral? Moral development theorists tell us the leader may have developed into an ethically reflective person as a part of

Table 4.1 Lawrence Kohlberg's Stages of Moral Development

Age	Stage	Substages
0–9 Years of Age	Preconventional	1. Avoid Punishment
		2. Gain Reward
9–12 Years of Age	Conventional	3. Gain Approval and Avoid Disapproval
		4. Duty and Guilt
20 Year + (or never)	Postconventional	5. Agreed Upon Rights
		6. Personal Moral Standards

maturing into adulthood. Research done by Lawrence Kohlberg (1981) and Carol Gilligan (1982) suggests that moral and ethical decision making becomes more sophisticated as a person develops from a naive child to a fully rational adult.

In Kohlberg's studies of moral development (1981) he applies Piaget's theory of psychological development to the development of moral thinking in children and youth. To Piaget's "preoperational/concrete/formal" distinctions Kohlberg adds a stage theory (summarized in table 4.1) to explain changes that occur in the moral and ethical reasoning of human beings.

For Kohlberg, the preconventional level of moral development is based on the cognitive abilities of a person in Piaget's concrete operational stage. Ego-centered and concrete, the child makes moral and ethical decisions based on self-regard (based on me). Reward and punishment are the most common bases of reasoning at this level.

Kohlberg's conventional stage is linked to the child's capacity to "de-center" his or her moral universe. Here the child is able to adopt the moral perspective of important adults (such as parents).

In the postconventional stage, the adult is able to base morality on the logic of decision making based on standards that are thought to be universalizable. This is a Kantian view of morality, and Kohlberg has been faulted for his bias toward Kant's rational actor model. Kohlberg's system is based on the survey and interview research he conducted with his students.

Gilligan's Feminist View of Moral Development

As Kohlberg's student, Carol Gilligan wondered why the findings of Kohlberg's research failed to match her expectations. She argues in her book *In a*

Different Voice (1982) that Kohlberg had left women out in his research! She proposes a stage theory of moral development for women.

Gilligan argues that Kohlberg's research questions focused upon justice. The fourth stage, for example, is about duty and guilt. Rule-oriented in its assumptions, Kohlberg's stage theory is biased toward explaining how boys and men think about moral and ethical dilemmas. Carol Gilligan counters Kohlberg by saying that girls and women tend to think about the "caring" thing to do, rather than the "just" thing to do.

In fact, Kohlberg's theory seems to regard women's thinking about morals and ethics as inferior to that of men. Gilligan did not believe women to be inferior in how they think or how their moral development proceeds. Gilligan did believe that they develop differently. The difference is that girls and women are more likely to focus upon human relations rather than the rules or laws. She created a fresh theory of moral development that amounts to the tracing of "an ethic of caring."

Gilligan's Moral Decision-Making Process

For Gilligan, men and women use quite different approaches in moral and ethical decision making. Most moral philosophers have been men, so women's perspective is considered to be less developed and sophisticated, or is not taken seriously, or is simply overlooked.

Gilligan begins with the view that philosophers (all males) believe that individuals have certain basic rights. Having rights and respecting those of other people are fundamental, and a moral system imposes rules and seeks to regulate what we can and cannot do. This is a justice orientation.

A female approach to morality argues that people have responsibilities toward others. To be moral is to exercise care toward others, morality is the imperative to care for others. Hence, the female morality has a responsibility orientation stressing duty and obligation.

Gilligan's Stages of the Ethic of Care

In table 4.2 we see that Gilligan's moral development model has three stages. The first stage is a selfish stage, the second contains a belief in conventional morality, and on the third, we reach a postconventional position on the ladder of moral development. In addition, there is progress here from a selfish concern to a social and principled morality. Gilligan believes female children start out with a selfish orientation.

Although females and males are both selfish at the earliest stage, generally speaking, the females learn to care for others. They come to believe that

Table 4.2 Carol Gilligan's Stages of Female Moral Development

Age	Stage	Goal
No Age Range Specified	I. Preconventional	Individual Self-Satisfaction
Transition—Selfishness to Responsibility to Others		
No Age Range Specified	II. Conventional	Self-Sacrifice
Transition—Goodness to Accepting Belief that She Too Is a Person		
May Not Achieve This Stage	III. Postconventional	Principle of Nonviolence/ Refrain from Hurting Others

being selfish is wrong. In their second, conventional stage, females understand it is wrong to act in terms of their own interests. They are convinced that they should value the interests of others. Here they avoid being overly concerned with themselves, seeing this as "selfishness." The third, postconventional stage, finds females believing it is wrong to ignore their own interests as it is to ignore the interests of others. This stage finds females reaching out and connecting with others.

Although her stages are like those of Kohlberg, Gilligan sees the shifts between the stages to be linked to changes in the sense of self. Gilligan's theory draws upon Freud's conception of the development of ego. She successfully combines the theories of Freud, Kohlberg, and Piaget. Hers is a theory that focuses upon changes in self-concept as well as the relationship of the self to the social setting.

Modeling Educational Leadership

The second way to become an ethical educational leader is to model those leaders and leadership traits and behaviors we see as successful.

Charismatic Leadership Model

For thousands of years, leadership has been identified with charisma. Caesar, Alexander the Great, Jesus Christ, El Cid, Mohammed, George Washington,

Napoleon Bonaparte, Theodore "Teddy" Roosevelt, Adolf Hitler, and Nikolai Lenin, to name but a few, were regarded as leaders because they drew people to them and convinced followers to believe in their visions.

One difficulty with charisma is that it may be completely irrational. Hitler and Lenin in recent history are good examples of leaders who mesmerized the people but whose vision was flawed. Charismatic leadership seems not to rely on the wisdom or counsel of other people, so the decision-making style is highly subjective. And charisma does not last; as with clothing fashions, people become tired of the same of thing.

Bureaucratic Leadership Model

The ancient Chinese philosopher Confucius (551–479 B.C.) set out the parameters for the bureaucratic leader. For Confucius, what was required was a group of wise, humane, courageous, and righteous administrator-clerks ("superior men") who could keep track of and guide the empire. Trained in record keeping and wise in the financial resources and needs of the state, these leaders fulfilled the role of modern accountants in school districts and universities. Watching the policies and money, they were able to control things in subtle but important ways.

Marshall, Steele, and Rogers (1993) review four versions of this traditional model of administration (rational, mechanistic, collegial, and political). Each is seen to push a uniform mind-set in which the administrative career is aimed at getting a better job at any cost. Leader-administrators do not use one of these models to the exclusion of others; typically, they may favor rational planning, fairness through equal application of policies and rules, friendliness, and achieving bureaucratic ends through conducting orderly meetings.

Leaders are believed to be effective when they are proper, serious, impersonal, and detached. They are considered "good" leaders if their communications are formal and hierarchical and they run a tight ship with stated goals and clear objectives, all of which are short-term and measurable. Bureaucratic administrators work with the structures provided and comply with professional codes and standards. During off-hours they work on their certification and licensure. As a result, educational leadership is often impersonal, and a gulf frequently comes to exist between the leader and the led. Most leaders with this bureaucratic mind-set are simply awaiting a promotion.

Servant Leader Model

New school leaders are apt to adopt the model of "servant leader." John Rawls, as a follower of Kant, finds value in this approach on the grounds that it is better to support just institutions rather than unjust ones. He feels we need to exercise mutual respect and mutual aid. Thomas Sergiovanni (1992) has advocated that the school leader be a "steward" to the school and its members. The servant leader is seen to be a product of an earlier "covenant" or sacred contract linking him or her to the goals and objectives of the school. Here a principal's main job is to facilitate and support the efforts of others in the school.

The Transformational or Radical Leader Model

Popular in the 1960s in Europe, Canada, Australia, Latin America, and the United States, radical leadership held a special fascination for college-age young people. In universities and colleges around the globe, civil disobedience was celebrated as the route to social change. Heroes were radicals like Tom Hayden and Abbie Hoffman.

This model of leadership casts the school administrator, teacher, or counselor in the role of change agent. The job of the transformational leader or radical leader is to make things different. The view assumes that some elements in the school or school district are in need of change. It further assumes that they can be changed and that a single individual can bring these changes about. It is taken for granted that members of the school community will go along with these change efforts. While this proposal does not on first examination appear radical or revolutionary, considerable barriers exist to conceiving of leadership in this way.

Disobedience, breaking with tradition, and even civil disobedience, may be a major feature of transformational or radical leadership. The radical leader is more likely to ignore laws and codes. While civil disobedience has had a long history (Henry David Thoreau, the American transcendentalist writer during the pre–Civil War debates surrounding slavery; Mohandas Gandhi and his battle for the separation of India from Britain; and the Reverend Martin Luther King Jr. and the Civil Rights Movement in the United States in the 1960s), as a concept it came to mean "Don't trust anyone over thirty."

Civil disobedience is an act responding to injustices within a given society. It is attached to an appeal to the public's conception of justice. Following John Rawls, we may see civil disobedience by the leader to be justified if the following three conditions are all met:

1. If there is a clear injustice, particularly one that blocks the path to removing other injustices. Serious infringements upon the principle of liberty and blatant violations of the principle of fairness in equality of opportunity would call for disobeying civil codes. For example, a practice that supports segregation in the school may be seen as a clear injustice.
2. The normal appeals to the majority have been made in good faith and have failed; civil disobedience is only a last resort. For example, a teachers' sick-out is a violation of the law, but may be justified in terms of a higher-order concern.
3. There are few other minority groups with similar, valid claims. If there are too many such groups, civil disobedience should be replaced by political alliances to form a working coalition (a majority). This route has been followed by teachers' unions throughout their history.

School leaders may adopt the role of the radical leader. Students or teachers may refuse to salute the flag or take part in ceremonies in school, or may dress or decorate themselves in unusual ways. Such expressions, when tied to higher moral principles and perceived injustices, need to be carefully weighed, and decisions must be made in terms of the interests of the disobedient and the institution.

For example, in the 1960s students and teachers began wearing black armbands to school to protest the war in Vietnam. These individual were often punished by expulsion or termination of employment until the courts began getting involved. It was deemed a significant victory for civil rights when armbands and other dress were allowed as expressions of individual and group disagreement. To forbid such dress was a marked violation of one's rights.

Reflective and Practical Leadership Model

Quite another model for leadership is the "reflective leadership" model revealed in the writings of John Dewey. In his books *How We Think* (1910), *Essays in Experimental Logic* (1916), and *Logic: The Theory of Inquiry* (1938), he laid out a viewpoint on thinking that departed significantly from older Aristotelian characterizations. Raup, Axtelle, Benne, and Smith, in *The Improvement of Practical Intelligence* (1943), written at the end of the progressive education era, encouraged teachers to adopt a model of "practical judgment" as they faced teaching problems. In the same book they also spoke of the "artist leader" as one who possesses aesthetic understanding. Judgmental skill was seen as a dimension of human moral/ethical character. And H. Gordon Hullfish and Philip G. Smith, in their work *Reflective Thinking: The Method of Education* (1961) lay emphasis on using ordinary logic.

For Dewey, the reflective teacher or administrator uses the methods of intelligent problem solving. Scientific and sensitive to the social issues of the day, the reflective educator is able to sort through the information, form hypotheses to solve a problem, select a course of action, inquire into its intended and unintended consequences, and test it out in experience. The good school leader is systematic in his or her efforts, yet open to doubt about holding all the answers.

Hullfish and Smith (1961) stated that "the role of educational leaders is, in essence, a teaching role" (p. 234). Here the educational leader is one who encourages teachers, students, staff, board members, and parents to participate reflectively in the activities of the school they share.

Reflective leadership is not manipulating a group of followers or giving orders so that people have no idea what they are doing or why. Principals and superintendents, to be reflective leaders, ought to liberate teachers and students so they may do their work. Teachers and staff possess enough intelligence to share in the exploration of new approaches to teaching and learning. Leaders ought to delegate power more often and share with faculty, staff, and students the forces and interests that are affecting the school and their chosen directions. The reflective leader is a facilitator, according to Hullfish and Smith.

In short, a school leader ought to examine the various models of leadership and decide which approach best matches his or her own style.

Crafting an Ethical Leadership: Design and Vision

As we have seen, we may argue that leaders develop into ethical individuals naturally; or they may adopt a leadership model; or they may extract ethical leadership from ideas about leadership with special attention to the moral and ethical values. Quite another way to see our path to ethical leadership is to construct it. Construction involves the skills of a craft, in this instance the skills of leadership.

Design

Leadership acts must be the "creative function," as Chester Barnard called it. Leading takes ideas and things, and makes them different through design and by forming and transforming them into the desired template of practice.

Admittedly the basis of all design is the interaction of self and the world. Dewey, for example, writes: "Interaction of environment with organism is the source, direct or indirect, of all experience and from the environment come those checks, resistances, furtherances, equilibria, which, when they meet with the energies of the organism in appropriate ways, constitute form" (Dewey, 1934, p. 147). Charles Taylor in his *Sources of the Self* (1989) characterizes a work of art as an "epiphany," by which he means

the locus of a manifestation which brings us into the presence of something which is otherwise inaccessible, and which is of the highest moral or spiritual significance; a manifestation, moreover, which also defines or completes something, even as it reveals. (p. 419)

Design is not identical to practice, for it is both elliptical and different. As a metaphor for the original it lacks the scope and detail of the original. As an artistic artifact, the design is not an action. Design may motivate practice, be incorporated into practice, be a vital part of practice, exemplify the heart of practice; but it is not reduced to action. Furthermore, design becomes worked out in practice. Design is practice insofar as one is engaged in designing in this sense of creating, rendering, or generating designs. Design in this latter sense is closely associated to *poeisis*,[1] as it points to a certain kind of knowledge of how to create something.

As an example, consider the school architect consulting with antiviolence and law enforcement experts in designing a school. With the norm of saftey in mind, the architect may borrow from airport construction practices and build restrooms without entry doors. Using models derived from motel construction, the designer may eliminate all blind corners and alcoves. Thus, when educational leadership draws upon design expertise in fashioning solutions of a technical nature to problems of an interpersonal kind, we have a fusion of the artful with the scientific.

Unfortunately, the tendency in modern administration has been to accept design as currently deformed praxis, or a practical/manual skill. Further, design has been mistakenly equated to simple implementation. For example, curriculum design has degenerated into naming a set of strategies for operationalizing un-reflected-upon "subject matter." School leadership and praxis are not matches. Leading calls for creative design rooted in values.

Design also has been tied down to the notion of structure. While art and artists are typically allowed divergence from the norms regulating space and material, design is seen to provide insight into already existent structures or to produce new structures. The implication is that design is about balance, harmony, reciprocal components, and so on: design yields construction.

Schoolhouses are typically boxes connected by hallways. The "windowless classroom" of the 1960s was an effort to force student and teacher to concentrate on learning by preventing them from looking outside. This design was a decided mistake, as the student's and teacher's attention was directed to getting to the hallways "to see what the weather was like outside." From a physiological perspective, it is wise to have a window nearby so that you can look away from the desk or computer screen and refocus your eyes. Such movements help strengthen the eye muscles and curb fatigue. Thus, it is important in designing educational spaces that the fuller knowledge of the physical and psychological characteristics of people be taken seriously.

A naturalistic or organic architecture could replicate plant forms, inspired by nature and yet going beyond. It is important to avoid mimesis, or the imitation of nature, a fault to be found in historical taxonomic classifications of learning by school psychologists. Design may be drawn from a variety of sources but express epiphanies by heightening and extending the value bases imbedded in school community. Values such as cooperation, collegiality, and shared decision making lie at the heart of educational institutions that succeed.

It is fruitful to examine design as it has played a role in other fields. When we look at the problems confronting urban planners, for example, it is clear that diverse methods and resources have been used in designing new urban centers. Planners draw upon art, architecture, policy studies, sociopolitical analysis, anthropology, and so forth to produce designs. Alexander (1987) writes: "Every project must first be experienced, and then expressed, as a vision which can be seen in the inner eye (literally). It must have this quality so strongly that it can also be communicated to others, and felt by others, as a vision" (p. 50). The *techné*[2] of the designer, while involving certain formal skills, also requires the perspective of the artist: the designer qua artist.

It has been suggested that skills and knowledges needed for urban design should be attached to the values and purposes of the people inhabiting the site; the analog in education is to be found in the sensitivity of site-based management as a set of designs to be matched to the "users being the choosers" (Alexander, Neis, Anninou & King, 1987).

Innovative school-building designs are regularly showcased in the magazine *Architectural Record*. What is interesting about such published examples of plans and illustrations is the changing concerns of the architects as the culture and society change. Our schoolhouse designs reflect our artistic values. The school boxes of the 1950s, the windowless classrooms of the 1960s, and the space-age buildings of the 1970s and 1980s all reflected the times. An excursion back to the first half of the twentieth century reveals the progressive educationists advocating schools situated in gardens. The assumption here was that the growth of children and the growth of plants were parallel and complementary. School gardens were designed to allow children to plant and weed the garden and thus feel closer to the organic nature of their own development.

In short, it is important to see design as not mere intuition of moral vision, nor technical knowledge, replication, or imitation, but as genuine artistry. The fact that artistic design deals with values reinvigorates the *quality* dimension of designs. Because educational design, as it emerges in leadership, deals with day-to-day management of institutional arrangements, there is a need to see participant reflective thinking bearing upon the design process.

No mere technical rationality will do here; what is needed is artistry marked by creative infusion of the human values of the institution (in this case the school). As Charles Taylor puts it:

> A human being can always be original, can step beyond the limits of thought and vision of contemporaries, can even be quite misunderstood by them. But the drive to original vision will be hampered, will ultimately be lost in inner confusion, unless it can be placed in some way in relation to the language and vision of others. (Taylor, 1989, p. 37)

Scientific-Reflective Thinking and Crafting an Ethical Leadership

Donald Schon's book *The Reflective Practitioner* appeared in 1983 and touched off a minor revolution in teaching, with many colleges and universities adopting some version of reflective teaching as their goal (Richardson, 1990). Reflective practice was not entirely new. As we have seen, John Dewey, H. Gordon Hullfish and Philip G. Smith, and R. Bruce Raup had written on this concept and paved the way for Schon's work.

Thus the belief that teachers ought to be thoughtful in their teaching is not entirely new. Not surprisingly, there is a real danger, given the history of concept-driven revolutions, that reflective practice may become just another educational slogan (Richardson, 1990).

As witness to the polysemous nature of the concept, at least three strong versions of reflective practice are operative in the literature:

1. Reflective practice as mediation of action assumes that new knowledge comes from experts (published) and that it is to direct and control future practice. This version of reflective practice stresses application of theory to practice. For example, the theories of moral developmentalism would be used to set up school experiments in which groups of students could be observed and their moral development recorded.

2. Reflection as deliberation among competing views takes for granted a plural and competing set of viewpoints regarding practice. The reflective practitioner uses a kind of "informed eclecticism" in choosing among alternative views to inform practice. Each alternative is considered relative to consequences, and the best option is selected. This version is a kind of interpretive knowing and is operative in the social studies. Instructional leaders present the competing views of the causes of World War I, for example, and then have the students work out the best answer on their own.

3. Reflection as reconstructing experience finds reflective thought to transform practice by (a) reconstructing problematic situations, (b) reconstructing self-as-teacher, and (c) reconstructing assumptions relative to the situation.

It is this last version that appears fruitful for the current crises in educational governance in the United States. Its critical stance owes much to Jurgen Habermas and his followers today but draws heavily upon an almost hidden tradition in American progressive education as well. The goal of reflection here is to liberate or reconstitute experience such that benefits are generated for human beings. This version seems to have much to recommend it for a new "critical educational administration." When we look to the research on reflective practice and educational administration, the sources are sparse and more evocative than scholarly. Aushbaugh and Kasten (1991) and Sergiovanni (1991) attempt to relate reflective practice to educational administration. Yet these efforts are hardly revolutionary and could well be conducted under a slogan other than reflective practice.

Of course it would be naive to assume that administration in general and management in particular have overlooked creativity and its bearings on organizational praxis. Chester Barnard early on sensed that leadership required an artistic touch:

> *The creative function as a whole is the essence of leadership. It is the highest test of executive responsibility because it requires for successful accomplishment the element of "conviction" that means identification of personal codes and organizational codes in the view of the leader. This is the coalescence that carries "conviction" to the personnel of organization, to that informal organization underlying all formal organization that senses nothing more quickly than insincerity. (Barnard, 1938, p. 281)*

Hence, the belief that practice in education, both as teaching and as management, needs to be reflective was noted historically. However, the degree to which practice ought to be reasoned, and with what kinds of reflection, need to be spun out.

Key Components of Reflective Practice

At this juncture, I should like to propose several key components of reflective practice and design for educators.

Habit

Habit forms a set of nonreflective practices that are, unless attended to, insulated from reasoning. Reflective practice is not habit. In the case of teaching and administering, habitual practices will become candidates for reflective reconstruction. The trick is separating the worthy candidates among habits from unworthy ones. Which practices ought to be reconstructed by thoughtful processes?

The bulk of human action will remain habitual in nature, relatively resistant to reflection. As Charles S. Peirce pointed out, it is only the introduction of a problem that breaks this continuity of habitual practice. Therefore, reflective practice emerges out of a problematic situation and the recognition that something needs to be done.

In the context of teaching and school leadership, doubtfulness about some educational state of affairs seems prerequisite for reflection. This contextual feature of reflective practice cannot be stressed too strongly.

Reflection

Reflection may be thinking about practice, but not necessarily rethinking practice. Reflective practice may be doctrinaire: a practice is justified where confirming evidence warrants the perpetuation of the practice. Popper tells us that theories are overdetermined by evidence: that is, everywhere we turn we seem to find confirming evidence for our pet theory. Rather than seek to confirm, we should attempt to reflect in a critical way. Thinking in the same old way about a teaching activity or administrative protocol would not qualify as reflective practice in this meaning.

Rehearsal

Attached to reflective practice may be the assumption that reflection follows upon practice. Clearly this may lead to a condition of too little, too late. If reflective practice is to be truly reasoned, attention must be paid to the anticipatory side of practice. We would be wise to think about likely outcomes before we engage in a particular practice. This is to introduce the pragmatic dimension to reflective practice, the side of it that faces the logical and real outcomes praxis generates.

Reconstructed or Reconstituted Practice

Any anticipated action may be subject to a reorganization in terms of data and conclusions. We may find earlier facts useless, with the conclusions faulty.

Retrospective

Reflective practice is also capable of being retrospective, in the sense that when we reason post hoc, we find the main difficulty to be assembling, interpreting, and organizing the evidence available to document a plausible case for criticism of a pragmatic inconsistency.

Self-Awareness

Practical reflection also requires self-awareness and self-understanding. Velleman (1989) tells us that your self-knowledge is your ability to explain what you are doing.

These features of practical reflection form a beginning (although incomplete) list. They indicate both the complexity and the significance of this concept as it bears upon school leadership. I wish to argue that a reconstituted form of leadership involves reflective practice, taken in this wider view.

Conclusion

While we may get our ethical leadership from either natural development or experience, that ethical rectitude may be enhanced through modeling certain leadership styles and designing our own moral and ethical leadership approach. Simply put, ethical leadership involves scientific reflection and artistic creativity to be successful.

Of course, practice is needed to become good at moral and ethical decision making. Moral character is a consequence of the repetitive moral and ethical decision making in which practical reflection and artful design are key components.

For ethical leadership to work, we need reconstructed notions of leadership and scientific reflective practice for educators, with stress on leadership as creative. Design is not a technical skill but an artistic effort to expose values. In the institutional setting of the school, a reflective practice is conceived of as an engagement with problems in need of reconstruction.

Notes

1. Aristotle classified knowledge as *theoria*, abstract and cognitive knowledge; *praxis*, practical knowing resulting from doing, arising from activity or development of manual skill; and *poiesis*, knowledge involved in making, producing, or creating some artifact.

2. *Techné* for Aristotle referred to anything created by humans in a deliberate manner. He sought to distinguish these creations from naturally occurring phenomena such as mountains and trees. A second meaning attached to *techné* is that of a skill or craft. A third meaning of the term specifically restricts its use to a knowledge of *how to do or make things* or *how to achieve a desired end*, or *how to produce* something. Fourth, *techné* also refers to the rational rules of procedure followed in making or doing.

5

Justice and Fairness in Decision Making

"Truth never damages a cause that is just."
— Mohandas Gandhi

Let us go back in time to the eighteenth century and consider the educational career of Johann Heinrich Pestalozzi. He was concerned about the poor orphans in Switzerland and decided to start a school to teach them trades and occupations. Pestalozzi was a loving and compassionate teacher and administrator. His school and teaching techniques (called "object teaching") caught on and spread around the world. Pestalozzi was the ideal caring educational leader.

Fast-forward to the early part of the twentieth century and St. Louis, Missouri. Superintendent William T. Harris was famous for his school system and his approach to teaching. Harris believed in discipline, structure, and orderly learning. Children should have their spirits "broken" and reshaped by the teacher. Harris favored a set of rules or principles by which each learning task could be taught. His ideal was the fair and equitable treatment of all students regardless of their special needs. The school was not to teach crafts or trades, or moral and ethical beliefs, but rather obedience to the state and its laws, and the common good above all individual goods. William T. Harris was the epitome of the leader committed to justice and fairness.

If we are to know the way to make leadership ethical, we must examine our attitudes toward ethics and morals, and the ways in which justice and compassion affect our choices in education are two of the most important of these dispositions.

We must detail the ways in which we talk and act about moral and ethical beliefs and practices when we think about our social or public spaces. How do we decide the just distribution of goods or services when such products are neither abundant nor accessible to all? How may we exercise compassion and caring? And what impact would a just or caring leader have on the school and pupils?

If the distribution of goods and services on an equitable basis would be harmful or underserve certain individuals, how do we justify rearranging our choices based upon our compassion for persons when compared with the common good?

John Rawls's Theory of Justice and Leadership

One of the most influential ideas in social science today is John Rawls's theory of justice. Rawls began work in the 1950s when two sets of theorists on morals dominated the scene: emotivists and cognitivists. The first group argued that all morals and ethics could be reduced to simple human emotion. No rational method or methods would ever be found to make sense of moral or ethical language. Therefore, we must trust in science and human reason, apply these to areas that lend themselves to scientific inquiry (ethics and morals do not), and begin the empirical work that is part of the human condition.

An example of an emotivist school leader might be the principal who becomes excited or upset whenever confronted or questioned. He is thinking with his emotions. So when he says that someone did the "right" thing, or that a certain act was "good," we can only conclude that this is an expression of his feelings and not a statement of fact.

On the other side of the fence were the cognitivists (utilitarians and intuitionists in particular). These thinkers held that ethics and morals were open to rational debate, and ethical behaviors and beliefs could be identified and embraced where they produced goods or stemmed from insight and curiosity (Wolff, 1977).

The school leader who analyzes every dilemma, breaks down the various positions in the debate, lays out the options, and in other ways operates in a scientific manner may be referred to as a cognitivist. Her techniques are based in intelligence and problem solving. However, she may express very little if any emotion. People call her "cold" or "calculating."

Rawls's theory of justice split these two views. His famous book *A Theory of Justice* (1972) continues to affect the social sciences and philosophy, and has deeper threads reaching into educational leadership and teaching theory. His work may be placed within the historical tradition of utopian and liberal welfare capitalist writings of the late nineteenth and early twentieth centuries (Wolff, 1977).

The Original Position

John Rawls developed a conception of justice as fairness. Imagine that you have set for yourself the task of developing a totally new social contract for today's society. How could you do this fairly? Although you could never actually eliminate all of your personal biases and prejudices, you would need to take steps at least to minimize them. Rawls proposes that you imagine yourself in an original position behind a veil of ignorance. Behind this veil, you know nothing about yourself, your natural abilities, or your position in society. You know nothing of your sex, race, nationality, or individual tastes. Behind such a veil of ignorance all individuals are simply specified as rational, free, and morally equal beings. You do know that in the real world there will be a wide variety in the natural distribution of natural assets and abilities, and that differences of sex, race, and culture will distinguish groups of people from each other.

In this original position, behind the veil of ignorance, what will the rational person choose? What fundamental principles of society will operate? For Rawls, the best principles will be fair principles. The individual cannot know whether she or he would suffer or benefit from the structure of any biased institutions. Therefore, the safest principles will provide for the highest minimum standards of justice in the new society.

To use a simpler example, suppose you are a member of a treasure-hunting expedition. You all happen upon a box of gold buried in the desert. What is the best way to divide the gold fairly among your group of individuals? One strategy would be to let the person who does the dividing of the gold receive the last share. This would lead that person to divide all shares as equally as possible in order to receive the best remaining share. Now, if the piles of gold coins were divided unequally, someone would get the largest share, but if you are the cutter, you can hardly rely on that piece being left over at the end.

Thus, Rawls begins by arguing that what we need to do is to think back to a time before there was a society as we know it. If we can imagine an individual person in such a condition, then perhaps we may reason our way to a more adequate theory of justice. He calls this the "original position."

The Veil of Ignorance

Next, he asks that we accept that individuals in such a position would not know whether they would in the future be wealthy or poor, healthy or sick, and so on. This condition he refers to as operating under the "veil of ignorance."

The veil of ignorance is a useful device because it eliminates self-serving in deciding the future social arrangements of society. For example, if I know that I will be wealthy in the future, then I will favor a social arrangement that protects this wealth. If I will be poor in the future, I will opt for a society in which there is a redistribution of wealth.

The Difference Principle

Rawls does not eliminate all inequalities by using these two devices, the original position and the veil of ignorance. Rather, he introduces a third, "the difference principle," which goes something like this: We might accept the unequal distribution of wealth in the future, if we were wealthy, if to do so would ensure that the lives of the poorest would be better. We might expect that there would be less likelihood of rebellion or revolt if the poorest people in society had some hope for a share of the goods of the society.

Rawls moves into ethics here when he proposes that we should, in his original position, favor doing no harm to others. He also assumes that we should in this condition favor keeping trust.

Reflective Equilibrium

The bottom-line recommendation is that we entertain a kind of "reflective equilibrium" as a society. This conclusion assumes some things about human nature and society. Rawls assumes that some people are committed to reaching agreement on important ethical decisions, rather than express different ethical conceptions. On the other hand, these same people do not wish one set of beliefs to dominate all others. The individuals in this society would be, he assumes, always committed to living together in one society. Finally he assumes that members of this society would accept that they must discover publicly stated principles and that these would be used in the future to resolve ethical issues (Nagel, 1999; Benn, 1998).

Rawls argues that all primary goods in a society (liberty, opportunity, wealth, and the bases of self-respect) should be distributed equally, unless an unequal distribution of any or all of these goods is to the advantage of the least favored. This recommendation was startling, but his reasoning kept philosophers busy for decades!

For Rawls, a person's good is equal to those things needed to achieve a long-term plan of life given reasonably favorable circumstances. In other words, a person needs liberty, opportunity, income, wealth, and self-respect. Thus, the good is the satisfaction of a rational desire. Rawls argues similarly that the rational individual would choose to establish only a society that would at least conform to the following two rules:

1. Each person shall have an equal right to the most extensive basic liberty compatible with similar liberty for others.
2. Inequalities of a social and economic kind are to be arranged so that they are reasonably expected to be to everyone's advantage, and attached to positions and offices open to everyone.

Two principles hold sway in Rawls's system of ethics: The "liberty principle" guarantees basic and universal respect for persons as a minimum standard for all just institutions. Yet, while all persons may be morally equal, we also know that in the real world there are differences between individuals. These differences might, under conditions of liberty, lead to social and economic inequalities. The second principle, the "difference principle," allows this condition and even suggests that it will be to the advantage of all to follow it.

In short, John Rawls provides a persuasive explanation of how leaders ought to exercise the justice idea in moral and ethical decisions. As a result of Rawls's work, we are clearer on how justice and fairness need to be appealed to in the moral and ethical dilemmas found in the school.

Distributive, Procedural, and Retributive Justice

It is not a simple matter to be just. We may exercise distributive justice in our moral and ethical decisions when we examine the outcomes. For example, if my decision affects a student's capacity to get a job, a teacher to gain promotion, and so forth, I am making a change in the context in which work is done. I am in fact distributing the goods of the school, district, community, or state.

Procedural justice calls for the leader to pay close attention to how decisions are made and whether they are made fairly. The decision-making process is held up to the light. For example, if the leader guesses at things or throws the dice, procedural justice is compromised. Persons interested in procedural justice are quick to see violations of due process in treating cases where morals matter.

Finally, retributive justice emphasizes punishment. The need for retribution is the need to reorient the goods in a group or community. It is not a long step to translating retributive justice into revenge. For example, a leader may determine that one of the teachers has done something so upsetting that the balance of power or privilege, role or position is changed. Punishment strips the person's recognition as a contributing member of the group.

Problems and Prospects in Using Rawls's Theory of Justice in the Schools

Tables 5.1 and 5.2, respectively, summarize positive and negative features of Rawls's theory as it can be used in the schools.

Table 5. 1 Positive Features of Rawls' Theory of Justice

1. **Fits Today's Schools**
   Rawls's view is liberal and rational. He accepts some of the assumptions of liberalism. For example, he feels that agreement will develop out of discussion, but he has strong ideas about what discussion is, and these ideas are modernist, twentieth-century beliefs. Finally, he uses rational methods to deal with moral and ethical conflict (Williams, 1985).

2. **Takes History Seriously**
   Schools never emerge in a vacuum: they always have a history. It is important for us in school leadership to attempt to situate our moral and ethical choices in an imaginative, historically determinate organizational culture, if we are not to overlook key variables affecting our decisions. Rawls's theory of justice is conscious of the historic development of social institutions like schools.

3. **Fits into Contemporary Interest in Tests and Effectiveness**
   Rawls follows the rules and expects others to do likewise, if for no other reason than it is in our best interests to do so. Schools across the country are focused on test scores and performance indicators. Justice criteria may be applied to the decisions regarding what to do when schools underperform. Increasingly, the state and federal courts will become involved in educational decisions. The legal model has a linkage with Rawls's theory.

Table 5. 2 Negative Features of Rawls' Theory of Justice

1. **"Small Is Beautiful"**
   From a school leadership perspective, one of the most serious difficulties with Rawls's theory of justice is its dependence upon size. He relies on an open public process of rational decision making that does not work well in larger institutions. As the social group gets larger, Rawls's working theory begins to fail. While Rawls's theory may work for small schools (like elementary schools in rural areas), the open and public feature of his plan begins to lose centrality as we take it to large schools, school districts, or state school systems.

2. **Public and Private**
   If we are to build upon Rawls's system, we must accept that modern schools have both public and private dimensions. Moreover, many decisions will have to be made in private or closed settings. While the open meetings rule determines how school boards must conduct business, it is far from clear that school superintendents, principals, and faculty must always make transparent the manner in which they have arrived at decisions.

3. **Back in Time**
   Another difficulty stems from Rawls's use of abstract language and ideal circumstances. We can never revisit his "original position," since this must have existed in prehistoric times. No record is left to us as to how people decided their fates in such times. Since schools cannot be assumed to have been part of the original conditions in prehistoric times, it is difficult to argue from such an original position to what school leadership ought to decide in particular moral and ethical dilemmas.

4. **People May Resist Redistribution**
   Rawls speaks in his original position of the distribution of goods as a kind of manna from heaven (as Nozick calls it) in an ideal society, yet we know that the *production* of goods in modern and postmodern society may motivate us to avoid the difference principle. If we have exerted labor in producing these goods, people might just not go along with redistributing them.

5. **No Theory of the State**
   Finally, Rawls has no theory of the state and no conception of political power (Wolff). This translates into a school context without any theory of the school organization within which to work out differences. Yet, we know that in the United States and other developed nations, schools are arms of the state, enforcing certain curricular and organizational matters set out by the legislature.

Taking the Best Parts of the Theory of Justice

The context in which justice is exercised (the school, in this) involves: (1) the space in which the individual affects teaching and learning, school governance, or other such matters; and (2) the resources of the unit.

In the first, personal identity, the unique features of the individual, are at play. How does leadership enable, empower, or in other ways advance the individual's self-respect or self-esteem? The aim here is to help people in the school feel good about themselves as they engage in social transactions with others.

When we consider justice to be solely connected with resources (money, honors, etc.), our focus may be on how these are distributed among the members of the group. Sometimes, by looking at reward structures and the amounts of money, time, or other resources available, we believe these allocations can be improved and the organization made more effective and efficient. Often, these decisions are not seen as involving morals or ethics. However, it is entirely possible for leadership to view the distribution of resources as a means to make the school more effective, yet have the opposite result as individuals come out with a less equal share of them. Sensing the unequal distribution of those resources, individuals may question their own self-worth. Followers are often quick to see resource allocation as a leader's means to reward friends and punish enemies. It is really misguided distributive justice or wrongheaded retributive justice, as it fails to make things better in the organization because it makes things more unequal. Alienating individuals who have been contributing adequately to the common goals of the school leaves the school less effective and the resources so unevenly allocated that individuals are actually hampered in their work. Soon the entire organization is in trouble (suffering from unethical moral space factors) because none of the distributive choices respect individuals and their contributions to the unit.

We need to ask if justice, as Rawls portrays it, has any gaps or fissures. If the aim of his system of justice is to make no one a winner, how can this be guaranteed? First, Rawls's system seems to overemphasize stability and duty. There certainly will be envy and jealousy in any social organization, yet to ignore this is an oversight. Rawls's system neglects these feelings. Everything must be rational for Rawls.

The priority of freedom (liberty) depends upon "progress." But what are we to do when school report cards reveal failure? Should we strip the school, its administrators, and teachers of their liberty? Self-respect and material prosperity are not handled very well here. Children speak about being "dissed" by others. Often they are disrespected because they do not have the same things the other children have. Capital accumulation of resources seems to override and determine self and self-regard.

John Rawls's theory of justice centers on two fundamental principles of justice that would, he argues, grant us a just and moral society, driven by a desire for fairness. The first principle guarantees the right of every person to have the most extensive basic liberty compatible with the liberty of others. The second principle is that all social and economic positions are to be open to everyone and advantage all.

Justice and the New Leadership Standards

The late twentieth and early twenty-first century liberal reform efforts in educational leadership rest upon the bedrock of Rawls's theory of justice. For educational leadership reformers the first task was to locate the "original position" of the institution of the public school in America. This was not difficult given that the history of public education was traceable to the first half of the nineteenth century and Horace Mann's public school reform efforts in Massachusetts. The notion that each citizen should be taxed to support a public school was supported by the fear that if children were not schooled, they would either compete with the educated employed or somehow turn into thieves and murderers.

Therefore, the leadership reforms hypothesized that schools must be dedicated to the redistribution of certain educational goods. Since people could not be certain (in the liberal future) that they or their offspring would not suffer from the influx of the uneducated into the labor market, and since such unlettered people could not make rational decisions in political voting, and since these uneducated persons might either compete for their jobs or rob and murder them, the reformers opted for a redistribution of the benefits of education. Motivated by fear that the poorest students would bring the entire society down, it was reasoned (difference principle) that some of the goods of public schooling must be redirected to the poorest students.

The Individual vs. Society

To support this decision, a mechanism for rational evaluation of schools, which treated them as if they were individual students, was created. Standardized testing of individual students leading to school report cards, school visits, and the evaluations of teachers and administrators were all used. Once the rational decision-making mechanism was in place, it was reasoned, the poorest performers in the system (now entire schools) could be identified and the remediation begun. Expert educators, an infusion of new money, and other devices were explored and used to bring the lowest-performing schools and poorest-performing students up to higher levels of achievement.

The difficulty for leadership in such a climate has been the historic rooting of educational administration in a nonegalitarian system with its tendrils embedded in elitism and privilege. The traditional nineteenth century pyramidal structure of school leadership, with the state legislature and state superintendent of schools at the top of the pyramid and the teachers and students at the bottom, already posited an unequal distribution of goods and power. Thus, once redistribution of goods was introduced in the late twentieth century, it became necessary to "restructure" or flatten the pyramid, setting each school against every other school to fit the new liberal principles guiding the redistribution of these educational goods (Maxcy, 1995).

Currently, there is a confusion between and disagreement over the principles or standards of leadership and the details of school reorganization. For example, we find emphasis placed on arguments about the nature and extent of effectiveness in leading schools, while at the same time political interests are fighting to have computers and connections to the Internet made equally available to all students. The conflict has moved the power of decision making from those originally entrusted with overseeing the distribution of goods and services for the good of all schools, to those most politically vocal about the need for those goods and services.

Once the standards for award are set, how shall we redistribute these educational goods to needy individuals, and what role will leadership play in this process? School districts seem committed to the principle of redistribution to the poorest-performing schools and pupils; this action is tied to the belief that equal resources will enable student test score performance to rise, thus solving our educational problems.

Unfortunately, the liberal solution to our concern about unequal effects of public education has resulted in pressure being placed on middle managers (school principals and assistant principals) to either get individual students to make their schools perform at higher levels or run the risk of having the school placed in receivership by the state.

Democracy and the Common Good

Philip K. Howard, in his book *The Lost Art of Drawing the Line: How Fairness Went Too Far* (2001), argues that we have sacrificed the good of most people for that of a few. He begins with the story of a children's slide being removed from a public park because it had been the cause of a lawsuit brought by parents of a child injured on the slide. He concludes that faced with individual rights and liberties, the common good disappeared. Americans are no longer able to draw a line between the public good and private harms.

Somehow the ethical leader must decide when an individual harm is so persuasive that it may warrant the removal of a general good. This choice is easier given the legal characteristics of Western democracies. After a few lawsuits, even the most steadfast defender of democratic commonality may give in. The irritation of a trivial lawsuit is often even a more compelling reason for giving up the common good in a situation.

Culture and experience set the parameters for moral and ethical decisions such that the common good was, as Enlightenment philosopher Jean-Jacques Rousseau argued, the most important good of all. In the twentieth century, the struggle for human rights turned the tables on the common good. Where groups were suffering disadvantages, it was deemed reasonable to persuade the majority to release its hold on benefits. The redistribution of goods based upon need or historic injury became all important. African Americans, the disabled, and women argued in courts of law that their special needs were being neglected in the pursuit of the common good.

Recent Trends: Social Justice

Since the 1960s our educational spaces have been the scene of a dynamic struggle to provide reforms in the name of social justice. Those groups who have been marginalized, have no voice, and in other ways have been treated unfairly came under critical scrutiny by reformers. Beginning with African Americans and their claims to desegregated schooling, and followed by parents of students with disabilities, Latinos, females, gays, and other groups, the effort has been to provide equal access, treatment, and social success through schooling. What the government and churches had failed to do, schools were told they must do.

The ethical school leader is taken to be someone who is sensitive to all the claims of groups represented within the school, knows and understands the sources and reasons for such claims, is disposed to honor them without hurting other groups or individuals, and still is pledged to the good of the school. With some inner-city schools serving five, ten, or fifteen different ethnic or other kinds of groups, this is a large order.

Moreover, the states, such as California, that early on had quite inclusive policies (e.g., the law that Mexican Americans must be taught in Spanish, and minority quotas must be honored in admitting students to the university) have backed away from such practices. As the culture becomes more complex and the issues more difficult, decision making has become most difficult. Fairness seems to be a elusive ideal.

Nevertheless, ethical leading involves the consideration of claims made upon the school, its resources, and its mission. Balancing evils, avoiding harmful policies, making exceptions, and so forth all seem to be ways in which leaders are navigating the rough waters of schooling. Being reflective, gathering information, exploring ethical theories and models of leadership, and generally employing the skills of sound decision making can help. Clearly, it is vital that ethical leadership be as practical as possible and that the leadership learn from decisions made in the past. New groups will emerge to make claims upon the school, teachers, and resources. Ethical leaders must be ready.

Conclusion

Rawls's theory of justice implies that for school leaders, moral and ethical decisions are matters of rational consideration and they are rooted in the belief that because we live and work in a society, we must consider other people's interests in making decisions. Rawls's call for fairness in treating others and their claims seems to be reflected in all kinds of educational sectors, for example in college admissions policies, athletic competitions, and scholastic awards. The danger is that by exercising leadership choices in the treatment of individuals and the allocation of resources, leaders may seek to reward their friends and punish their enemies. Under the guise of equity and efficiency and effectiveness, the school space becomes a place in which it is less equitable to teach and learn. Hence, while the common good is the overriding consideration in Rawls's plan, individual contributions and rights are considered less important.

6

The Caring Attitude in Ethical Leadership

"Always do right—this will gratify some and astonish the rest."
— Mark Twain

Until relatively recently, educational administration was dominated by men. Logical and rational, male leaders often stopped short at speaking of "caring" or exercising compassion in directing organizations like schools. Yet teachers (mostly females) had a historic investment stretching back to the 1820s in caring for children and youth. Two attitudes, one for men leaders and the other for women teachers, came to be the norm. All this changed in the last decades of the twentieth century. Educational leadership began to be spoken of as a caring profession.

The caring attitude has made its way into educational leadership in two ways: First, it has resulted from the recruiting of many more female elementary, middle, and secondary school teachers into university educational administration preparation programs. These females who already possessed the caring attitude in their teaching brought a regard for empathy with them into university school administration training programs. While such preparation programs had been filled with men students in the 1940s, 1950s, and 1960s, the profession changed in the 1970s. Many men found other, better-paying jobs outside of education; they abandoned school administration for greener pastures. Only very recently has the balance of female to male students begun to restabilize as men come back into the school administration profession. Still, in 1999, 64 percent of the doctorates in education were awarded to women (Chronicle of Higher Education, 2001). Allied with the infusion of females into administration preparation programs was the gradual opening of the educational administration professorate to women (McCarthy, Kuh, Newel & Iacona,1988). Curriculum and teaching methods became more empathic and caring as more women were granted doctorates and females became professors of school administration in the universities (Beck et al., 1997).

Second, caring invaded the profession of school administration through shifts in elementary, middle, and secondary school employment patterns. Beginning in the 1970s, more and more women became certified as school administrators and began taking posts in the schools, often beginning as assistant principals (AP). In the vast majority of schools the AP was the disciplinarian. Male APs were tough, rational, and no-nonsense leaders who demanded respect and dutiful behaviors from the students. Female APs could operate in a more caring way toward students because of their gender. After all, they were teachers who had moved into "the office."

The prejudice against caring school leadership was still strong: many of these female APs never rose to become principals. We have seen how prevalent the just and fair approach to leading has become. Linked with the "rational man" mode made popular by philosophers since the time of Immanuel Kant, reasoned decision making has dominated as the hallmark of proper school command.

The caring attitude, found most often displayed by assistant principals rather than principals (Marshall, Steele, & Rogers, 1993), has led to the "career assistant principal," or the leader who, because of caring behaviors, seems to telegraph the message that she or he does not aspire to be a principal. When Marshall, Steele, and Rogers (1993) examined male and female career assistant principals, they found them to display feminine characteristics like placing people before the organization. Like their male principal colleagues, caring APs were capable of treating people in an open and fair manner. However, the APs were more willing to listen and to dialogue, wishing to develop relationships with students and teachers. Intuitive, trusting, persistent, sensitive, and thoughtful, APs seemed to be striving for holistic meanings, plural ways of doing things, and relativity, continuity, and connectedness in their experience. In short, the AP was more caring (Marshall, Steele, & Rogers, 1993).

The impact of caring upon career leaders in schools has been formidable. APs do not get promoted to become principals if they are too caring in the previous role. Why is this the case?

Different Readings on Caring

Feminist Readings of Caring

Clearly the most interesting work on caring and schooling has come from feminist thinkers. Carol Gilligan (1982) and Nel Noddings (1984) seek to develop an ethics of care that is tied to the essential female tendency to be a caregiver in Western cultures. Placing female caring as a primary trait takes form in at least three strong theses.

1. *Biological.* The biological thesis claims that certain innate biological factors determine a person's morality (Ferguson, 1977). Differing moral qualities are attached to male or female biological nature, which determines moral behavior. Female biological traits are assumed to be caring, kindness, unselfishness, and so forth.

2. *Sociological.* The sociological thesis proposes that social or cultural factors determine a person's morality. Environment, family, and sociocultural context set our moral behavior. One version of this thesis states that the most significant cultural phenomenon is gender.

3. *Paternity.* Finally, the paternity thesis argues that women's caring morality is different from men's because it has been imposed upon them by men. This domination theory sees men dominating women, and women aiding in this domination by adopting a caring approach. The upshot of this thesis is a tendency to introduce revolution as a means to break the bonds of conditioning and generate freedom for women to make moral choices (Almond, 1988, pp. 51–52).

Grimshaw (1986) points out that although Freud has been criticized for sexism in his theoretical writings, he is at least half correct when he identifies females as having a different approach to moral and ethical matters and that this difference is rooted in a differing psychic development (p. 187). Some writers have criticized Freud's error in thinking as yet another male telling females they are overemotional and implying they are deficient in their moral and ethical development relative to men. But Freud is only incorrect in seeing the female approach to morals and ethics and their differing development as inferior to that of the male. It is the impersonal nature of his views that disturbs us.

An essential tension emerges here: If we accept the premise that females by virtue of their biology are caregivers and men are not, then how may caring be a means to equal treatment in what has been a male-dominant social system (Fisher & Tronto, 1990)?

Grimshaw (1986) proposes, an essentially "female ethic" that (1) assumes gender differences in the ways we approach moral and ethical issues; (2) offers ways to describe these differences; (3) asserts that female approaches ought not to be considered inferior to male approaches; 4) proposes that women recognize male approaches to ethics as damaging and dangerous (p. 194).

But feminist ethics has a larger agenda than merely accounting for gender difference in morality. At the heart of feminist ethics, and hence an ethics of care, is the wish to challenge the hegemonic nature of male ethics and to insist, as Pearsall (1986) tells us, on "the woman's voice" (p. 266). This is to say that feminist ethics emerges out of women's lives and interests. Certainly, the important controversies surrounding abortion in recent years highlight this special focus. Reproductive rights are seen as priority rights of females, but without the sanction of a male ethic. Recasting arguments in the abortion and stem cell controversy from a female ethical perspective therefore reveals the essentially liberating nature of caring for females: care for one's own body over that of others; care for those least able to care for themselves over the empowered ones.

Finally, feminist readings of ethics have had an enormous impact on schools and leadership. Since the 1970s, female philosophers of education have been cautioning educators to look at ethics from a gender perspective. Textbook writers and curriculum experts began using examples from women's biographies, poetry, essays, and other accounts to exemplify the importance of female ethics for young girls. And, in general, educational leaders are more aware of the gender difference in morals and ethics than ever before.

Critical Theory Readings of Caring

As a collection of thinkers, critical theorists have had difficulty understanding the language of feminism (Ingram, 1990). There seems to be a further parting of the ways between critical theorists and feminists as they view caring. The tendency of critical theory is to accept Kohlberg's Kantian-inspired developmentalist view of ethics without question and dismiss Carol Gilligan's feminist theory of a caring ethic as irrational and unsubstantiated.

While both groups argue that cultural and social conditions are repressive, critical theorists tend to rest their views on formalistic, universalistic moral theories that are insensitive to the "genderized other" (Ingram, 1990, p. 207). Critical theory suggests that within the rise of technology and bureaucracy are aspects of late capitalism that carry with them the decline of traditional institutions. Locked into a logical empiricist or positive science motif, school administration has overlooked the role of social norms and values in its institutions like schools.

Sensitive to the need to resist efforts to reproduce the unequal conditions in the social world, critical theorists have also believed that the public sphere (which includes schools), rather than the private space of family and close friends, is the arena where moral and political thought and reform are conducted best. What is critical for the critical theorist is not caring but rather the need for rational methods and the raising of questions of legitimacy in researching school-based problems.

Practical Readings of Caring

There is a third route to understanding the place of caring in educational leadership and ethics. It is found in the work of twentieth century philosopher John Dewey. Dewey seemed to enjoy locating two polaristic positions and then finding a middle ground or compromise between the two extremes. This strategy seems fruitful here.

While a just attitude may be needed in certain circumstances, a caring approach may work better in others. Rather than beginning with one basis for ethical decision making such as justice or caring, the practicalist proposes we begin with the moral and ethical situation. Allowing the situation to dictate the best attitude has the advantage of being less abstract and remote, more ad hoc and practical. Also, practical school leadership is more focused on the results than the rational or emotional processes employed. What will my decision based on compassion and care result in for this particular group of people in this setting?

Less dedicated to transformation and liberation than genderized and critical theory ethics, practical ethics is concerned that ethics be rooted in experience. If a child is in a wheelchair, should the physical education teacher force him to "dress out" for class? If we are prone to take the attitude of justice, the answer may well be "yes." The same rules for all students, regardless of their limitations. If we are approaching this problem with a caring attitude, it may be "no," yet the child may well benefit from at least putting on the school T-shirt and feeling a part of the class.

Just as we ought not to treat people solely in terms of categories or groups of which they are members, it is wrong to look to our emotions and feelings, blind to their particular affiliations or individuality. Practical ethics means we look both at the individual, the group, or clique, and at the situation to generate our decision. While too often we settle for statistical groupings or feelings of family resemblance in locating devices for alerting us to disadvantages, numbers may also blind us to caring about the individual child.

Practical ethics calls for a healthy view of the circumstances as well as the needs of individuals and groups to form decisions. We will learn in short order what the meanings of justice or caring may be relative to concrete circumstances and our decision.

Positive Features of a Caring Leadership Model

Caring has come late into the kit bag of educational leadership. Changes in culture and employment patterns have moved caring to center stage, where it competes with rational and prudent decision making. Educational leaders ought to know more about caring as an attitude and how it works in making moral and ethical decisions. The following are some of the positive features of the caring attitude (also see table 6.1).

Meets a Human Need

Marshall, Steele and Rogers (1993) argue that there is a basic human need for security and attachment. Caring as an ethical leadership strategy fits women best, owing to a biologically based primal or natural need to care. This is not to say that men do not care, but that it is less predominant in male leadership. If women have a human need to care, then caring should be allowed into the arsenal of attitudes of the ethical school leader.

Celebrates a Gender-Specific Attitude

Sociologically, gender appears to have some influence in determining a person's morality (Almond, 1988). To demonstrate a caring attitude is therefore deemed socially better understood and accepted for a female than a male.

Expresses Women's Voice

Some experts (Pearsall, 1986) argue that caring as a function of feminist ethics marks women as different and provides a part of "women's voice," which has been largely unheard in cultures.

Enhances Effectiveness

Caring and its measurement can be superimposed upon the current research literature on effective schools. The battles, for the practical ethical leader, are not to be fought out on the field of abstract criteria or competition among theories, but rather in the rough-and-tumble of the classrooms. Lightfoot (1983) argues that effective school principals in one study exhibited certain "feminine" qualities such as nurturing, receptivity, and responsiveness to contexts and relationships. Levine (1990) seems to agree that school administrators, to be effective, must possess certain characteristics that are feminine in nature.

Celebrates the Individual

Caring, to be legitimate, should be concerned with individuality, individualism, and individuation. This is to say that caring, to pass the test, must demonstrate service to the individuals involved (caregiver and care recipient). Hence, some solid theoretical basis for so conceiving individuals is essential to our understanding of what caring is all about.

Table 6. 1 Benefits of a Caring Approach to Ethics

1. **Caring Is a Human Need**
   Females may have a basic human need for security and attachment.
   Caring as a leadership ethics disposition fits women administrators better than men.

2. **Focus on Relationships**
   A caring approach focuses on relationships and not specific acts or behaviors.

3. **The Ethic of Care as Contextual**
   The caring approach to ethics works best in a small and familiar school context.

4. **Works Best for Career Assistant Principals**
   The caring model works best for the "career assistant principal."

5. **Caring as Effectiveness**
   Effective schools researchers point out that effective schools exhibit certain "feminine" qualities, among which is caring.

6. **Caring Celebrates the Individual and Women's Rights**
   Caring is concerned with individuality and difference.

Possible Problems Facing the Caring Educational Leader

Is it possible for an educational leader to be too caring? We all know of cases where teachers or administrators have become so involved in a student's problems that their own work and lives suffered. Just as the psychiatrist must be wary of becoming absorbed in a patient's difficulties, so too must the educational leader seek a balance between being a helper and being a fellow victim. (See table 6.2 for some difficulties associated with caring.)

Caring: Moving from the Private to Public Moral Space

The caring attitude seems to carry with it certain innate difficulties. First, caring is often directed at family members and one has difficulty abstracting caring to the world at large. There is a tendency to make decisions based upon the most proximal members of society (family, kin, clique, etc.). Concerns for starving people in other countries do not carry as much obligation as sickness among family members. Next, caring is an attitude and it is not clear how one teaches an attitude. There may be individuals who are systematically unable to care (owing to injury, etc). Thus, the mechanism of caring is not a stable way to deal with the day-to-day ethical choices.

The most difficult task for any theory of caring is to move from the private to the public moral space. Undifferentiated and abstract caring is difficult to maintain if we try to accelerate our concern for family and friends to large groups of people. And it is in the public sphere that principles come into play. Hence the fundamental difficulty facing a disposition to caring is to move from individual to plural without sacrificing caring for some other attitude. While we can seemingly justify our regard for family or kin, it is not easy to justify caring in general.

There is little means for moving our leadership ethics as it assumes the attitude of caring for family, friends, and local individuals to a scheme of compassion for the larger public.

Personal Responsibility

Noddings's caring conception does not demonstrate how to decide on personal responsibility to fulfill general social obligations. This responsibility for a wider public is an obligation that defines an individual's moral and ethical identity (Neville, 1989, p. 11). The circle within which the individual operates is local and parochial, and as such impoverishes his or her capacity to think and act on more global concerns. Claudia Card (1991) and others have argued the caring person seems not to have the capacity to consider people in foreign lands in problematic situations of his or her own making. The localized caring philosophy has no place for the proximate stranger and hence is incapable of crossing political and social barriers of gender, race, and ethnicity—seen as interests—to promote sociocultural change.

With so many students coming and going from schools, the transient student faces a problem of invisibility for the caring leader.

Caring as a Power Relation

Rather than confronting and attempting to overcome power relations, caring invariably splices our caring interpersonal relations and colors our communicative efforts. Where nurturing and care become primary, the play of power over the field of transaction/interaction is significant.

The primary issue here is not school leader effectiveness, but legitimacy. If we are seeking to impose a practical test, caring in the context of education should be exercised so that it is nonoppressive, nondominating, and thus nonefficient. Caring conceived of as a part of a power relation calls for legitimate exercise and must be freely authorized (Rouse, 1987, p. 250). We ought not to be compelled to care, but rather come to our caring as free sentient beings.

Caring as an attitude, to be an acceptable power relation within a school, must be tied to standards or principles. However, these principles have most commonly emphasized some kind of contractual relationship or the greatest good for the greatest number (Rouse, 1987). At this level and functioning as a kind of social agreement, caring seems to require public support and not private reciprocity. If school leaders need to ground caring on results or charters and contracts, the short-term and local good that caring can accomplish is diluted or destroyed.

Caring and the Moral Act

What is the nature of the moral act? Caring fails to tell us the answer to this question. We have no dependable way to link care as an attitude to moral and ethical leadership. I may do good things for people, without caring for them. I may continue to care long after the cared for ceases to give any demonstrable response (e.g., grieving for dead relatives).

Caring seems to be a localized and small-group phenomenon (like family mores). But we are interested in the larger life of the school, the community, and the society. Most caring strategies lack this capacity to account for the larger group or national character. We must ask of caring, as an ethical explanatory conception, how it accounts for an ethos or national character.

No Prohibitions

The study of law demonstrates that attached to any inclination or desire we may have, there is probably a prohibition. Thus, it is possible for one to "care too much." What is the prohibition on caring? As a school leader, if I care about a student, I must also have some way to limit or extinguish that care. Without a prohibition, we have no way to check for excesses. Caring turns to obsession. For example, we have all witnessed teachers or administrators who appeared to care too much. They were so focused on one student or one problem that things got blown out of proportion. If the difficulty were not resolved, they tended to mull over it excessively, upsetting their personal lives as well as their professional work. We need to have some way to check too much caring, and that may be the adoption of other attitudes to replace it. For example, the attitude of temperance, or justice, or a concern for the good of the entire school, may help to reduce the stress and tension of caring too much.

Caring as Communicated

Most desire philosophies neglect the role of the desirable. Rationality enters here. A student may desire something, but only because some teacher has convinced him or her that it is desirable. Desire is communicated. Caring is similarly brokered: I care because I have been told to care, encouraged to care, taught to care and so forth. Here the caring may be a function of reasoned discourse. I come to care because I am convinced of the good reasons why I should. Caring in this way may become part of moral education.

There is also the trap of thinking that "being just" or "caring" are merely feelings. As the emotivists tell us, we ought not to base our decisions on raw emotions. Attaching my ethical act to a guiding attitude like caring may seem to absolve me of responsibility: it is not I who is responsible for this particular ethical decision, but my attitude, and it was the wrong one for the situation. For example, we would have little sympathy for a principal who failed to call

---

Table 6. 2 Difficulties with the Caring Attitude as a Basis of Leadership

1. **From Private to Public**
   The caring attitude works best when the leader is dealing with family, close friends, or neighbors: It does not work well in dealing with abstract groups or situations.
2. **Focus on Relationships**
   A caring approach focuses on relationships and not specific acts or be-haviors, therefore it does not fit in with today's standards-based school leadership models.
3. **The Ethic of Care Is Contextual**
   The caring approach to ethics works best in a small school settings.
4. **Works Best for Career Assistant Principals**
   Caring works best for the "Career Assistant Principal," who has no desire to be promoted."
5. **Men Make Women Caring**
   Men, through their dominance of women, have forced females to be more caring. Women leaders accept this responsibility, and therefore reinforce this power relationship.
6. **Caring Is Not Just**
   Caring be not be capable of being used to provide equality of treatment in a male social system.

---

police when a student pulled a gun and held a teacher hostage because he "really cared about this student." In such a circumstance the appeal to law and justice is best.

Taking the Best Parts of the Caring Attitude

As we have seen, there are a number of good features for having a caring dis-position as a dominant leadership attitude. Caring has been a central attitude in education since at least the fifth century B.C. Socrates, Plato, and Aristotle each emphasized the necessity of a loving relation between teacher and student as a preface to learning. As contemporary society becomes more technologically driven and more impersonal, we find distance between our-selves and others widening. Caring for others restores something that is vitally human to the equation. How can we promote caring in educational leadership?

Visualization

It is often helpful to picture a school situation or dilemma that requires you to have a disposition to act. When you have the facts and values in hand and are examining the options for the decision, it is a good idea to try to visualize how your choice will affect the people involved. By mentally walking through your decision and how it may be received by the students and teachers affected by it, you can better calculate the strength or weakness of a decision.

Picturing a good school is like having a vision of, if not a program for, improvement of the conditions in the school.

Caring Sensitizes Us to Oppressive School Conditions

Following Fay (1987), caring helps us see the oppression of others. Caring in the larger educational arena never rests lightly on our shoulders. Almond (1988) tells us that "the ways in which women's lives differ from those of men are indeed morally significant." She goes on to argue that "the feminist goal must be the interweaving of those values, which have a richness, complexity and spontaneity lacking in more abstract conceptions, with the universalistic goals of traditional moral theory." Almond seeks the creation of the new morality that "must in the end be a joint enterprise of both women and men" (p. 56).

Culture Shapes Caring

We learn to care, not in any rational way, but rather through subtle and not so subtle absorption and refractions of our culture and experience. The acts of caring, the many ways in which caring is characterized in our culture, arise in transactions with the family, street, and school spaces. The attitude of caring and the disposition to exercise care are in themselves learned, but only partly through an education involving novels, poetry, lectures, and other creative instruction. We may argue that becoming a caring person, adopting a certain set of considerations, in which the body centers the responding being to be open to another, is the result of almost surreal conditioning. To gain these predilections is part and parcel of becoming a certain type of body/mind in this particular culture at this time.

Within today's school spaces the attitude of caring is assumed and therefore is neither given recognition nor encouraged. Caring is supposed to come with the territory and with the teacher's craft. Yet, unless caring is nurtured and developed, rewarded and encouraged, it will not prosper for long in the harsh reality of our schools.

Recent Trends in Caring: Obligation

One emerging trend finds caring being abandoned for feelings of duty and obligation. As parents age, their adult children may begin with a feeling of caring and move to a feeling of obligation. Caring and love are replaced by duty and a sense of responsibility for our aging parents. As a culture matures and becomes more conservative and less willing to experiment, ethics swings toward a greater concern for obligation than the free-wheeling rights and privileges of a youthful time. Today, we see the media and the schools caught up in a wave of effectivism and standards. This press for accomplishments and achievement is placing more responsibility upon children and adults for the way things are.

What had been entitlements and free by virtue of our status in a society are now set in a context of achievement and striving. Welfare has been replaced by work programs, law enforcement is seen in terms of jail terms, school learning is equated with test scores, and so forth. We can thank the philosophers Thomas Hobbes (1588–1679) and Immanuel Kant for fostering today's social contract theories of ethics and our culture's embrace of obligation. According to Hobbes and his followers, modernity ruled out the divine right of kings and natural rights of individuals. Despite all his searches, Hobbes could not find any objective moral values. Kant was less sanguine. He argued that certain principles or maxims could be located. Kant's famous notion was, "Act only on the maxim through which you can at the same time will that it be a universal law." While Kant believed a good will was the only unconditional good, he tended to focus on rationality and the measured search for principles of ethics to determine how this good will was defined.

Thus, while all are dedicated to pursuing their own ends using whatever means they can secure, and while harming another person is not morally wrong, it opens one up to being harmed in turn. Therefore, Hobbes and Kant reasoned that people enter into social agreements or conventions (social contracts), bargaining for mutually advantageous conditions. Individual human beings are naturally equal from the start but do tend to compete, according to Hobbes. Rights come from the constraints needed to maintain a mutually beneficial cooperative community. Hobbesian and Kantian contractualism assumes we have no natural need for expressing a caring attitude toward others, but we do have an obligation or duty toward others.

Shift to present-day educational philosophy and we see a Hobbesian or Kantian social contract at work in many social contexts. For example, educational authorities and agencies (school district, state department of education, federal government, etc.) push individual educators, students, parents and the public at large to believe that their right to education is accompanied by an obligation (or number of obligations) to believe and do certain things. For example, the right to attend a free public school is matched with the obligation to learn what is taught and to perform well on high-stakes tests. As individual students strive to learn and pass tests, they must become cognizant of other students and their needs as free and equal players in the social contract.

A caring ethic focuses upon love and affection for the other. Traditional male ethics like that of Hobbes and Kant emphasize social arrangements functioning through the mechanism of obligation. Today, schools stress less the love of learning and the positive relationship between teacher and student, and more the value of achievement and winning. We have moved in schools from an ethics of aspiration to an ethics of duty.

The core value of good leadership and good schools is heart. By putting in place dispassionate social contracts in the schools, rooted in the values of duty and obligation, and by embracing minimal standards and thresholds of performance for students, teachers, and administrators, reformers have compromised the lives and futures of our children and the careers of our educators. It is not too late to reverse this course.

Conclusion

In this chapter we have discussed the caring attitude and how it may be used in ethical educational leadership. We have learned that caring has its positive and negative aspects. As good practical ethicists, we have chosen to seek a middle ground between justice and caring, allowing the situation to dictate the approach we feel fits the circumstances.

Finally, as ethical leaders, we may be better off putting caring in with other moral and ethical attitudes and dispositions, such as a concern for justice and human rights, a regard for the common good, and a desire to do the least harm. We may similarly argue that having courage, temperance, prudence, or honesty are at least as important as having a caring attitude. In the pages to follow we will examine these other attitudes and their importance to leadership ethics.

7

Science and Ethics

> *"A moral being is one who is capable of
> reflecting on his past actions and their motives—
> of approving of some and disapproving of others."*
> — Charles Darwin

The Problem Science Poses for Ethical Leadership

"Should the theory of evolution be taught in our schools?" "Ought we to use public money to fund university scientists as they use human stem cells in their search for cures for Alzheimers, diabetes, and spinal cord injuries?" "Should students perform dissections of animals in high school biology labs?" "Should sex education be a part of the curriculum?" These questions and others call for decisions but require more than "just the facts" to make them. They are moral and ethical quandaries and at their heart they reveal a commitment to competing theories of social and cultural change.

Educational leadership aspires to be a science, and in this pursuit, the importance of ethical and moral values often disappears. In the spirit of logical empiricism, educational researchers have sought to locate "facts" about school leadership and to teach them to budding administrators. The quest for certainty transformed school administration into a science wanna-be.

Until the seventeenth century and the work of Pierre Bayle (1647–1706), ethics and religion were one and the same. Introducing a wedge between science and religion, Bayle wrote in 1682 that many orthodox Christians were murderers, thieves, and rapists, while plenty of freethinkers were of the loftiest character (A. G. R. Smith, 1972). If an atheist could live a virtuous life, then moral choice and ethical character had no necessary roots in organized religion. By the second half of the nineteenth century Sir Charles Darwin pushed ethics into the lap of science.

Today, in large measure, questions surrounding ethical dilemmas have their roots in biology. The Human Genome Project is uncovering the hidden biological genetic factors beneath our strengths and weaknesses as a species, while ethicists are debating the potential for doing harm to people through informing them of deadly illnesses captured within their genes. While the struggle of scientists now is to locate the organic sources of physical differences in the development of humans, the nineteenth-century intellectuals sought to discover how things in nature came to be the way they were (Hofstadter, 1970). What is missing today is the means for understanding educational leadership and individual and social change through more sophisticated and more adequate social and cultural theories. Our science no longer matches our theory.

In the nineteenth and early twentieth centuries a template for a new scientific view of ethics was created. The bearings of new morality had a profound impact on leadership and social institutions like schools.

No scientific pronouncement more upset the ordinary lives of citizens in the Western nations than the introduction of the theory of biological evolution, set out most systematically in 1859 by Sir Charles Darwin (1809–1882) in his book *The Origin of Species*. Darwin prompted a shift in how we were to think about humankind's place in the grand scheme of things in the mid-nineteenth century, and today. What most upset the ordinary citizen was the challenge evolution set for religion. For followers of Christianity in particular, evolution contradicted the Bible in significant places. How could God have created the world in six days, if its species have been changing according to the laws of evolution? Do we follow God's law or follow the evolutionists?

It is not surprising that John Scopes, a teacher in Tennessee, would be the test case for whether Darwinian evolutionary theory would be taught in the schools. The famous "Scopes trial" took place in the heat of the summer of 1925. Two famous lawyers argued the case, William Jennings Bryan and Clarence Darrow. Darrow defended Scopes and sought to prove he was on solid scientific grounds in teaching biological evolution. Bryan told the court it was all blasphemy and that the Bible was the authority. Scopes lost the case, but Darrow's arguments shook the religious communities in America. The biological record was seriously challenging the accepted religious accounts of the origin and development of the natural world.

But it was in the hands of one of Darwin's followers, Herbert Spencer (1820–1903), that the relationship of biology to ethics was to have its deepest impact. Spencer, one of the fathers of sociology, crafted a pervasive doctrine of "the survival of the fittest" (Hofstadter, 1970). This singular idea of each person competing with every other had such a widespread effect on Western nations that it continues to color our beliefs about leadership and to underwrite many institutional decisions of an ethical nature.

Thus, although one way we are influenced by evolution is through the experiments, discoveries, and teaching of evolution, it was via key social philosophers called Social Darwinists and their critics, through their reconstructed systems of cultural and social history, that future personal and social development was changed.

Biological evolution emerged as a problem for ethics in the nineteenth century when certain social philosophers sought to apply research evidence and findings to fund a large-scale theory of biology: the transfer from evolution of organisms to evolution seen as human cultural and social development. The question about the relationship, if any, between biological evolution and human morality grew out of the historic efforts to interpret the biological theories of Charles Darwin for human social and cultural history. On one side were the evolutionists, who believed that there was a mechanism of transformation within nature that accounted for changes in the shape and function of living organisms over time. The other camp was populated by antievolutionists, who believed no such mechanism existed, but rather God created creatures and their universe at one time, forever to remain the same. The fundamental disagreement came to pivot around what was meant by "change."

Change is a central challenge for education, also one that must be addressed full-face by the educational leader. No school would be accomplishing its implicit aim were it not dedicated to change; changing ignorance into knowing, weakness into strength, desires and emotions into cool-headed thought, or changing small children into adults. The issue has come to be what template we as educators embrace to explain which changes are good, how such changes take place, and whether they can or cannot be taught.

The battles over the place of evolutionary theory in the teaching and practice of biological and geological sciences might have been all that mattered were it not for the leap of faith that took evolution into the social and cultural arena. Although Flew (1967) tells us, "The obvious and the right place from which to begin a study of evolutionary ethics is the work of Charles Darwin" (p. 1), the better place is with the theories of Herbert Spencer. When he spoke about education, he argued that leaders were born, not made; ethical choices had to maximize the survival of the fittest right down to the curriculum and the teaching of science as most contributing to survival.

A second way in which biological evolution affects our contemporary posture toward ethics in general, and education in particular, is through criticisms of Social Darwinism. In the later 1880s, a second group of social philosophers emerged who sought to contradict this Social Darwinism. Seeing Spencer's theory as largely a political version of Darwinism, Thomas Huxley, Friedrich Nietzsche, and Henri Bergson made attempts to construct moral and ethical theories that took biological evolution seriously, yet sought to improve on the Spencer brand.

Although this second group differed among themselves, they nonetheless offered up fruitful intellectual critiques of Darwin's theory and its fittedness to human moral life.

The Gang

By looking at the unit of the tribe or gang, Sir Arthur Keith argues in *Essays in Human Evolution* (1946) that such communities have always struggled for survival against one another. Within each tribe or gang, however, the "ethical cosmos" strengthens social bonds that allow members to cooperate as if they were a team. Thomas Huxley, however, saw evolution or the cosmic process in terms of individuals in a struggle for existence, and the ethical process as counter to this cosmic process. Keith, as he interprets Darwin, finds the struggle for survival and the ethical process to be "consistent elements" of the evolutionary process (p. 3–5).

For Keith, the tribe is taken to be an "evolutionary unit," with biological integrity exhibited in shared genetic autonomy. The tribe insulates itself against other tribes, with members bonded through common territory and kinship. Nature, in addition to creating biological unity, has also developed "tribal mentality." This mentality operates in two ways: first, it acts "intra-tribally," in the sense that it serves the welfare of the members through the good or virtuous aspect of human nature; and second, it is inter-tribal or extra-tribal as it acts with enmity toward other tribes. Keith sees this last type of mentality to be good from an evolutionary point of view, but evil from a systematically ethical perspective (p. 5).

To demonstrate his theory as valid, Keith selects the example of Nazi Germany. Historically, he tells us, Germany began as a multitude of tribes that evolved by using warfare. The Third Reich resulted from this process. The evolutionary means used to bring this unitary dictatorial state about were war, force, terror, and propaganda. Given the end they created, Keith feels the Nazi use of evolutionary means or methods are "from an ethical point of view, immoral" (pp. 6–7).

In short, Keith views evolution as an intertribal struggle for survival, with success a function of tribal integrity and instinctual cooperation. Ethics applies only to members within tribes, with "the good" being that which serves social welfare. Also, the concern for social welfare is a given of human nature. Tribes as they interrelate operate in accord with the evolutionary biological principle of survival of the fittest, which from a moral standpoint is an evil; within tribes, the members are guided by human ethical codes whose purpose is to promote social solidarity. Both spheres are nonetheless within the cosmic process and subject to the laws of biological development. Finally, through human manipulation via ethical codes, humans may change their biological future (pp. 5–6).

The tribal unit view represents a more traditional Social Darwinist position. It supports ethnocentrism (belief that one's group is superior to all other groups) and chauvinism (belief that one must fight for, or defend, the tribe against its enemies). Tribal evolutionism makes loyalty appear to be identical to moral virtue. What needs to be sorted out are such matters as regard for one's tribal ethical codes and regard for higher, cross-tribal standards. In educating for ethical character, children who are taught only these tribal codes may fail to achieve higher levels of morality. Conflicts would emerge where attempts are made to reform or reconstruct tribal ethics to meet new social needs. A true evolution of ethics would be impossible. Choices would be reduced to one level (and a lower one for Kohlberg). A trans-valuation of values would become impossible given Keith's view.

Shift focus to the school. As early as 1943, with the publication of August B. Hollingshead's *Elmtown's Youth*, and William F. Whyte's *Street Corner Society*, the role of gangs in adolescence gained educational researchers' attention. Today, urban schools are being territorialized by gangs in every city across the nation as well as internationally (Vigil, 1988). Students join to-gether as they find things they have in common ("we hate the ____" or "we all are ____"). Being a member of a particular race, ethnic group, or socio-economic strand may serve as a stimulus to form a gang, often because students desire identity or status in a space that makes this difficult or im-possible. Wearing certain clothing, jewelry, tatoos, or colors serves emblem-atically to signify affiliation to "the brotherhood" or "the sisters."

For the school leader the Latino, Vietnamese, Chinese, or other gang can be a moral and ethical nightmare! Faced with competing gangs, the school space turns into a fully contested battlefield where all students suffer the pos-sibility of harm. What is the school leader to do?

First, following the tribal theory of evolution, it is important for the edu-cational leader to realize that students will join groups, particularly in ado-lescence. Seeking things and beliefs they hold in common with others in their age group is a powerful driving force for most adolescents. Psychologists tell us that this stage in development, particularly in the past seventy-five years, has been a difficult one for a child. With biological features in seeming re-bellion, and uncertain of who they are or what they will become, adolescents naturally seek certainty and safety in the group. Rebellion against adults is a natural feature of this stage of life in today's modern and postmodern cultures around the world. "Acting out" is a known result of not knowing what or who they are.

Second, the moral leader needs to communicate. The adolescent dilemmas are serious and in need of dialogue. Talking with them about their emotional and intellectual desires and fears is vital to adolescent students. The school leader must not only have an open door, but must go outside his or her office into the corridors and streets to seek out students, to talk within neutral spaces.

Finally, the moral leader needs to be committed to helping students af-filiate in positive and significant ways. The "Crips" and the "Bloods" are fic-tional gangs from the musical *West Side Story*, but they exist in fact in many inner-city schools. The school leader should not be defensive or put off by the tribal values expressed in her school, particularly middle school. Students who are undergoing biological changes will also experience a transformation of their development in values and beliefs. Just as tribes love or hate their leaders, adolescents are most sensitive to leadership in the school.

Moral school administrators must therefore be *consistent*. Tribal members operate with a large core of central values surrounding their beliefs about the value of the group and what distinguishes it. Treating the gang or its members unfairly or capriciously is suicide for the school leader. Every gesture and action of the adolescent gang member tests the sensitivity of the adult to them as a part of something sacred. In many ways the tribe and gang are metaphysical units that may fail the test of scientific explanation.

Finally, the moral school leader facing a tribal culture ought not to violate a *confidence*. Complaints about the gang, a member, or another gang lead to mistrust. Few adolescents will confide in a leader-adult who "rats" on them, or in other ways violates a confidence.

Leadership, Ethics, and Control

If science, through its arm of biological evolution, provides the explanatory heart of the gang, ethics found in many schools today may also offer clues to how we may counter destructive tendencies within such groups and redirect their ethical choices.

It was largely in response to the efforts of Herbert Spencer and his follower William Graham Sumner (1840–1910), the champion of private school education, that the principles of "cosmic" evolution were applied to the sphere of human ethics. Thomas H. Huxley, in his book *Evolution and Ethics and Other Essays* in 1896, became the spokesperson for a science of ethical control.

Huxley tried to counter Herbert Spencer's "survival of the fittest" notion by stressing that laws and morals work as restraints upon the biological struggle for existence. Ethical standards were taken by Huxley to be historically in opposition to the evolutionary biological development of humans, where this transformation is seen as a survival struggle. The best qualities for such survival, Huxley believed, had been suppressed by the moral dimension of society (Huxley, 1896, p. 31). He made a fundamental distinction between the products of humanity and those of nature, as well as the developmental processes that accompany each sphere of production. For Huxley, humankind is changing as part of the cosmic process, in the sense that humans are evolving like other biological organisms; however, graced by the unique factor of intelligence, humans are capable of shaping their own future development. Huxley found human development and cosmic biological evolution often to be at odds (p. 11). He saw a natural antagonism between biological evolutionary means and human social ends.

Society is a work of human art, originating out of organic necessity, Huxley believed. But this human society is different from animal society in the fact that there is no predetermined role in society for individual members. Human society can be contrasted with bee society, for example, which finds its members created with predetermined roles. In addition, humans possess a desire for pleasurable experiences and a genuine distaste for painful ones. For Huxley, this pleasure-seeking is a given in humans that society has tempered and restricted to promote social ends (p. 27). Thus, humans are restrained from unlimited pleasure-seeking by the sanctions of the group. Furthermore, shaming as a technique serves to punish moral wrongdoers, while honoring rewards the morally straight (p. 29). Human conscience is an acquired characteristic that checks the natural proclivity for pleasure-seeking, while promoting acts that contribute to social welfare. The development of moral conscience Huxley referred to as the "ethical process" (p. 29).

Pleasure-seeking could be ruinous for a society, yet excessive restraint of such pleasure-seeking could be equally damaging. Human sympathy, if allowed to influence societal sanctions, could nullify their effect, Huxley argued. Huxley assumed that the criminal naturally seeks to avoid punishment, and that if societal sympathy is too great, the group would refrain from punishing, thus leading to more crime. A balance must be sought, Huxley believed, between the wishes of the individual and the welfare of society.

The notion of the development of human society toward some state of perfection, as Spencer had predicted, was incorrect for Huxley. This ideal end condition would deny human desire for self-assertion and pleasure, and perfection would also undermine the human basic intellectual fallibility. In addition, the interests of single members of society would always be in opposition to those of the group or gang. Hence, the evolutionary development of biological life (the so-called cosmic process), having as its purpose the supposed survival of the species, will necessarily be at odds with the development of restraint and societal solidarity. These factors are counter to the biological struggle for survival, Huxley believed (pp. 41–49).

The cosmic process is "a scene of strife, in which all the combatants fall in turn" (p. 49). The most obvious characteristic of the cosmos is impermanence, while its greatest product is the human being seen as a member of an organized polity (p. 51). Through superior skills of survival, the human species has risen to the position of biological leadership in the biological evolutionary world (p. 52). Owing to self-assertion and success in struggle, humans have developed from savage to civilized. Organizational and societal talents have contributed to human success in the struggle to survive.

The crucial question for Huxley is whether there is a sanction for morality in the ways of the cosmos (p. 80). His answer is that there is no such sanction. The progress of society operates as a check upon the cosmic process by means of a human ethical process. The most biologically fit of organisms no longer need necessarily to survive: rather, the more ethical members become candidates for the "fittest" category viewed from a human perspective. The virtuous person is then not the cosmologically fittest, for the simple reason that she or he eschews ruthless self-assertion in favor of a cooperative and dutiful attitude (pp. 81–82). The ethical progress of society depends upon combating nature (i.e., the cosmic process). Humans subdue nature for their own higher ends.

In sum, biological development simply has nothing to tell us about how to be a good human being. History has been the tale of human restraint and modification of the cosmic process through reason. Morality has arisen in human society and has no relationship to biological evolution except to oppose it!

Given Huxley's view, students of ethics desiring to become leaders are not better off for studying the patterns of biological evolution. If we seek to instill moral and ethical ideals in ourselves and students, more can be gathered from a study of society and culture than an investigation of cosmic evolution. This is in part due to the problems of scale. Cosmic processes involve such macro changes that they have no significance for micro events in human lives.

Insofar as a curriculum of moral education is concerned, units dealing with great individuals in history or crises in politics would provide the sort of evidence needed for children to learn of leadership and ethics. While Spencer would probably agree to a *laissez faire* approach to the teaching of morality and ethics, Huxley would not. For the latter, the major interest is the development of cooperation and the study of demonstrable evidence that humans have countered cosmic evolution in their rational ascent to humanity. The "fittest" would not be the triumphant athlete or the infantryman, but rather the morally superior individual (such as the Reverend Martin Luther King, Jr., or Mohandas Gandhi).

Implications for the role of the leader as ethicist for schooling are far reaching. First, it is taken as fact that the school as a social institution is a product of the finer side of human nature. Rather than struggle and warfare of all against all, the school is the by-product of cooperation.

Next, according to John Dewey, writing in *The Influence of Darwin on Philosophy* (1910), and Lester Frank Ward (1841–1913) in *Dynamic Sociology* (1911), society evolved, not so much as a result of conflict but owing to the application of human intelligence to inherited (often organic) conditions. Through collaborative and conjoint efforts, human beings with similar interests and goals could redirect inherited instincts and habits so as to cast new futures. Morality was reflective in the sense that it did not rely upon hidden "cosmic" biological dynamics of certain kinds; however, it was sensitive to the evolution of humans because there were limits upon human flesh.

The Superman and Ethical Leadership

The superhero ranks high in Western culture. Superman, the Hulk, Wonder Woman, Spiderman, Spawn, and a variety of look-alikes have dominated the comic books and movies for decades. On the football field, basketball court, or wrestling mat, superathletes entertain millions of people on a regular basis. Americans in particular love their heroes. Most often, the superhero also exercises superethics, saving the poor and defenseless or winning the game for "the Gipper."

The importance of the superhero and the limits of small group ethics, advocated by the Darwinists, were first highlighted by the German philosopher Friedrich Nietzsche (1844–1900). For Nietzsche, there was a likelihood that human moral ideas would be a danger for the biological development of the human species. Nietzsche undertook a strong critique of Darwinism and a critical scrutiny of the origin of ethics as a means for determining the value of human morality. Making a significant distinction between the value of a moral idea and the intrinsic worth of such morals, Nietzsche pointed out that the worth and value of morals had been assumed uncritically (pp. 153–155).

Historically, the concept of "good" originated among the nobles and ruling class, which viewed itself and its actions as good because they were in opposition to a lower, dependent class of individuals referred to as "bad" (p. 160). Nietzsche saw the term noble to mean good, while *common* or *plebeian* meant bad (p. 162).

Ethics underwent changes in a second evolutionary stage, Nietzsche claimed. It was during this shift that aristocratic leaders became synonymous with the priestly class. This amalgamation plus a clash with the warrior caste caused an inversion of the ethical code of the nobles. More specifically, Nietzsche believed the Jews were responsible for making the poor and powerless class "good" and the nobles "evil." The Jews, Nietzsche argued, were responsible for the "slave revolt in morals," in which the ethics of the common person came to prevail over that of the nobles (pp. 167–168). The slave rebellion arose out of a rancor against the rulers and was a response to an outside stimulus in the form of a moral code. Thus, hate gave rise to a slave ethics, while noble morality resulted from a triumphant self-assertion upon the part of the aristocratic class (pp. 170–171). The noble-minded individuals created the notion of "good" and derived from this concept the notion of "bad"; however, the low-minded originated the idea of "evil" to refer to their enemies, the nobles. These two sets of valuations, the nobility's "good-bad" and the slave's "good-evil," have through the ages done battle, with the result that the slave morality has gained ascendancy (p. 188). Throughout this historic period, schools reflected this division in language and social class.

Two sets of moral ideas evolved, according to Nietzsche. These moral sets were related to biological evolution of human organisms. The ethical standards of the lower class, as they operated to promote survival of the weak, were less valuable than the moral ideas of the nobles, which aimed to promote the survival of the few (p. 188).

The term guilt for Nietzsche arose out of the notion of material indebtedness associated with the marketplace. As Nietzsche put it: "It is in the sphere of contracts and legal obligations that the moral universe of guilt, conscience, duty . . . took its inception" (pp. 196–203). If the debtor were unable to pay a debt, the creditor could inflict pain upon the debtor, thus gaining pleasure commensurate with his loss. In short, the feelings of guilt and personal obligation arose in primitive times out of the personal relationships between buyer and seller. Indebtedness began to prompt feelings of guilt. With the growth of communities, the group came to operate in the role of the creditor, while the individual criminal assumed the role of the debtor. Societal punishment came to work in the same way as the primitive creditor-debtor relationship in the case of forfeiture. Inflicting pain fulfilled the same purpose in both instances (pp. 196–203)

Nietzsche saw the development of a slave moral code into a universal sovereign system to be contrary to life's biological purpose. Legal codes became a weapon of the rich to thwart the biological and evolutionary struggle for power, which can only result in human demoralization and the elevation of nothingness (p. 208).

Biological and social evolution took place in a sequence of processes. These processes were sometimes individual and sometimes collective, and at times progressive or regressive. At all times, the processes were an expression of the will to power directed toward the goal of increasing the strength and perfection of the class of persons as a whole. In fundamental disagreement with those who held that adaptation was the mechanism of most importance, Nietzsche believed that the very essence of life was aggressive, self-assertive, spontaneous individual action (pp. 210–211).

Speaking from a scientific and psychological point of view, Nietzsche saw the evolution of human society to be the cause for the "bad conscience" found in people. Given the biological need for aggressive action, and the fact that society restricts such action, humans developed bad conscience to punish themselves. Once this guilt was gotten rid of, humans then seized upon religion to further the torture. To Nietzsche, such a course of action was an insanity of the will, since it was the will having lost its aim (i.e., self-assertion) that had resulted in an empty goal. That void, Nietzsche was convinced, was the "ascetic ideal" (pp. 225–231). The ascetic ideal was the opposite of the vital instinct, in the sense that it was a psychological wish to be different from life. Christians, and especially priests, were responsible for elevating the void of the ascetic ideal before humanity. The whole process of aspiring to the ascetic ideal signified for Nietzsche a hatred of humanity: a "will to nothingness."

Schools, often housed in churches during the Middle Ages, reflected this aesthetic ideal. Much of what we regard as the seven liberal arts was laced with the goal to rise above one's biological status as a human organism, and to become a saint. Only with the collapse of Christianity and the end of its ethic would there be a release from the insanity of the will, Nietzsche asserted (p. 299).

In sum, Nietzsche held to the notion that there were two types of morality based on class distinctions: slave morality and master morality. From an evolutionary point of view, Nietzsche saw the moral codes of the masses to be in opposition to the biological evolution of human life; the master's morality, with its emphasis upon individual self-assertion, is in keeping with the progressive development of the human species and will necessarily lead to the strengthening of the fittest and creation of more powerful groups.

Tracing the practical bearings of Nietzsche's moral philosophy to the leadership of schools, children and youth must be viewed in a new light. Teachers must teach students the historic nature of morality and caution them to embrace the master morality of the leadership, rather than the conventional slave morality of the lower classes. To teach master morality would be to show the true evolution of ethics in biological terms to be a function of historic class antagonisms.

1. *Superhero Morals.* Properly educating children and youth in the master morality would produce a generation of the *ubermensch* or "overman" or "supermen," Nietzsche reasoned. Such super individuals (either male or female) would come to dominate the new world order.
2. *Emotional Chaos Into Order.* These young people would have organized the chaos of their emotions. Superheroes restore order and bring law to ungoverned situations.
3. *Character.* Through education and experience, youth would develop strong characters by experiments in moral reasoning.
4. *Creativity.* Finally, the moral superman would exercise creativity. Unlike the slave exercising a morality riddled with guilt, the ubermensch would use a master morality to build a life for himself.

"Do It for the Good of the School": The Ethics of Social Solidarity

During the worst times of Soviet Russia's control of Poland and other Eastern European countries, the cry for "solidarity" could be heard as a revolutionary slogan. Certain groups of Polish revolutionaries and others wished, through the means of joining together, to counter the doctrinaire policies of the Russians. Social cohesiveness or solidarity has been a clarion call for improvement, success, happiness, and a host of other goods over time. In education, solidarity is often touted as a "natural" mechanism for restoring harmony and the good life through teaching or school reorganization. Solidarity as a function of biological instinct has serious moral and ethical implications for school leadership.

Solidarity had its biggest fan in Henri Bergson (1859–1941), a French philosopher of evolutionary theory, who was deeply influenced by the writings of both Charles Darwin and Herbert Spencer. Bergson was in fundamental agreement with Nietzsche on the point that there are two distinct kinds of morality, but for Bergson the morality of obligation has its sources in society, while the morality of aspiration is extrasocietal in origin. For Bergson, human beings derive a morality of obligation from society in the sense that the individual acting out of habit seeks to promote social solidarity. In an analogous way, Bergson sees society as if it is a biological organism. Individual members operate like the cells of a social organism. Beneath this first type of morality lies the notion that instinctual social obligation fosters a "closed society," in the sense that it has a finite, local concern regardless of humanity at large (Bergson, 1935, pp. 1–32).

The Morality of Obligation

The morality of obligation results from a biological instinct transformed into habitual action with its goal being the preservation and perpetuation of society. Hence, this first type of morality fits into the biological evolutionary scheme (p. 55).

The Morality of Aspiration

The second kind of morality, the morality of aspiration, finds intuition and revelation to free humans from the limits set by biological nature. This morality arises from individual imitation of exceptional humans who seek to conform to the interests of all humanity rather than mere societal needs. This form of morality is strongly reminiscent of Nietzsche's "ascetic morality," yet unlike Nietzsche, Bergson sees such moral behavior as ideal. Whereas the morality of obligation carries with it the element of power and force, the morality of aspiration is guided by an appeal. Furthermore, the morality of aspiration is instinctual, while the morality of obligation is learned. The morality of aspiration is superior to the obligatory morality owing to the fact that it leads to an open society, Bergson concludes (pp. 34–39; 57).

Thus, Bergson sees Nietzsche's scheme and probable consequences to be deemed more valuable. In so doing, Bergson rejects the Kantian "categorical imperative" and the fundamental principle of human rationality that undergirds it. For Bergson, reason can only put forth reasons, but behind rationality is to be found the exceptional human who, functioning as a model, has drawn us toward the ideal open society based upon the universal brotherhood of Man. Hence, the morality of aspiration is beyond reason—it is the morality of love (pp. 65–66).

Bergson felt that humans as living organisms have evolved under the impulse for greater organization, while societies have evolved under the impetus for social solidarity. The unique feature of human evolution relative to the evolution of other species is that at some point exceptional individual members of Homo sapiens have appeared. These unusual human beings, sensing the kinship of humans, have sought to break the societal barriers through love (pp. 94–97). This unique "impetus of love," Bergson sees as the creative dimension of evolution that has transformed the human species. Thus, both kinds of morality reside within the evolutionary scheme of things (pp. 96–97).

These two types of morality have existed historically. Ethics is intimately related to biological evolution, in the sense that it promotes either social solidarity or humanistic ideals, Bergson believed. For Bergson, there are two distinct lines of evolution: the instinctual, which leads humans to sacrifice themselves for the welfare of the society; and the inventive intellectual evolutionary line, which leads individuals to change society.

Closed and Open Society

Just as there are two kinds of morality, for Bergson, there are two types of society (pp. 111–115). The movement from a closed to an open society is promoted through the mechanism of religious dualism. While "static religion" has historically preserved social solidarity by means of myth-making, dynamic religion has transformed society through mysticism. Hence, Bergson's "creative evolution" consists of a dynamic mystical leap beyond the status society rooted in obligatory morality (p. 257).

The educational implications of Bergson's work are quite different from those of the Social Darwinists.

Ethics of Love

Rather than survivalist knowledge, children are to be taught the ethics of love, as well as a regard for a morality of aspiration, according to Bergson. Bergson's theory of ethics assumes the role of God and love to be essential for everyone to live life successfully.

Open Society or School

Bergson's viewpoint favors the open society (or open school) with free discussion by all. It envisions the triumph of reason over raw nature. For Bergson, evolution must be "creative" and aimed at achieving higher levels of life through an "impetus of love."

Cooperation

Students taught according to Bergson's philosophic view would not be encouraged to compete but rather shown how to cooperate and to aspire to more noble standards of rational ethical behavior.

Rationality

These youngsters would be shown how to thwart the more instinctual types of actions in favor of the more rational behaviors necessary for a civilized existence. Using reflective thinking will lead children to make rational decisions about right and wrong.

Bergson's philosophy of ethical leadership led the way to an "ethics of care." We see Bergson's philosophy as a warrant to reconstruct education and leadership following a cultural evolutionary model.

Subjectivism: Praise, Blame, and Leadership

Some ethicists have believed that upon inspection every society and culture operates according to two human emotions: praise and blame. Edward Westermarck (1862–1939), the Finnish sociologist and anthropologist, was an ethical subjectivist. For Westermarck, all ethics arises from two human emotions: moral approval (praise) and moral disapproval or indignation (blame).

1. *Moral Approval (Praise).* Moral approval, or praise, is a form of "retributive kindly emotion," Westermarck argued (Westermarck, 1932, pp. 60–67). For example, a science teacher picks up the test papers of his students upon the completion of the examination. He observed two children exchanging answers in the back of the room during the test. The next day, he returns all the test papers, each marked with an A. This praise has a positive effect on the students who earned their grade, as well as those who cheated. The teacher, following Westermarck, believes that each person has his or her own meaning for right and wrong, and since no one is really correct, he simply rewards everyone in the class for effort. The teacher may rationalize his judgment by saying that it did not make any difference anyway.

2. *Moral Disapproval (Blame).* Moral disapproval is a form of resentment for Westermarck. If the same science teacher were to grade the two students who cheated with grades of F, he would be expressing his feelings about their behavior. He would disapprove of what they did. This feeling is an equally

acceptable one for him, and he would be perfectly correct in grading the two students down. Feeling disapproval, the teacher would have to rationalize his decision. The better the reasons, the better he will feel about his choice.

Rejecting the notion of some moral theorists that moral emotions are a consequence of but never a cause for moral concepts, Westermarck proposes that emotions cause moral judgments. Furthermore, moral judgment is subjectively valid for ego, in the sense that ego sees the judgment as applicable to all similar cases, whether ego may participate in judging or not. Westermarck adds that ego may feel no emotion and yet be motivated by such emotion. Moral concepts are words that contain intrinsic tendencies to bring out moral emotions of approval or disapproval (pp. 60–67).

The development of morality consists of the increased use of rationality in judging moral matters. Although all moral judgments are based upon emotion, variations in moral judging arise when people hold differing conceptions as to the nature and consequences of actions. Thus, for Westermarck the biological evolutionary model is useful in explaining how ethics improves, in the sense that humans become more knowledgeable concerning the nature and results of their judgments. This is not to say that the source of ethical pronouncements changes, however, for Westermarck believes that the emotions will always have a primacy in ethical judgments (pp. 71–72). Morality is evolving as human rationality becomes more and more adept at justifying ethical judgments and in understanding the nature and results of ethical choices (pp. 70–72).

How does a subjectivist perspective, like Westermarck's, affect educational leadership? There are two ways, presented in the following sections.

Subjectivists and Standards-Based Leadership

The first way leadership is supported in certain ways by the subjectivist is to see standards functioning as rules or benchmarks resulting from human emotion. For example, a subjectivist might argue that the ISLLC Leadership Standards grew out of the progressive disapproval of leadership performance in the schools. Once the standards are in place, judgments about how school leaders must act can be made. But, since such standards have their source in the human emotions, we ought not to take them as laws. Nor are we warranted in evaluating the school leader's performances too harshly. After all, emotions may lead to a variety of actions, some good and some bad. The performances we like today may be unpopular tomorrow.

The role of standards-based leadership does not require the ethical subjectivist to do anything but rationalize the decision. "I chose to expel the student caught decorating his third grade teacher's car with flowers, because he swore at me in my office!" Subjectivist leaders are most sensitive to their own comfort and the role they have in the school. Few have sympathy or concern for others' feelings. By the same token, if a teacher makes an ethical decision about a student, the moral and ethical relativist principal need not accept her reasons. Since he engages in rationalizations and excuses, he believes everyone else does as well. Subjectivist ethical leaders view every moral and ethical choice in terms of how it affects them, not other people.

Westermarck would advise the standards-based leadership advocates that every school administrator will simply seek the moral approval of superiors. Every moral and ethical choice would be as good as anyone else's. Fixated at the "good boy," "good girl" developmental level, they are incapable of ever making moral and ethical choices based on reason alone.

Moral Education

What if we start early and teach children to be reasonable in their ethical judgments? Will this strategy prepare them as adult school leaders to exercise rationality in their ethical decisions? Not really!

A second way to see subjectivism operating in schools is as a developmental stage of immature students. Westermarck would be similar to Lawrence Kohlberg in his acceptance of stages of moral growth from irrational to rational. Individual moral judgments would be studied and reason used to determine the appropriate decision. However, while Kohlberg believed the child could be taught for the next level of moral development, thus aiding his decision making, Westermarck would never accept the higher levels of moral development as realistic. The lower reaches of ethical decision making would rest on emotion, but more high-minded moral choice would be a function of rationalization.

Children could not be taught to make better (more scientifically reasoned) ethical choices or to avoid the emotional effects on their judgments. Westermarck's bias is in favor of the individual person, and not society. The open versus the closed society is a moot question for Westermarck and would have no bearing on adherence to leadership standards or moral instruction in the school. Thus, we have in Westermarck's view of ethical leadership a conviction that all morality is subjective; it is not based on reflective thinking, but on emotion. Finally, for the subjectivist, you cannot inquire into moral and ethical dilemmas or approaches used to solve them because these efforts will never yield objective truths.

Naturalistic Ethics and Biological Evolution

Naturalistic ethics improves upon subjectivism by starting from the belief that moral and ethical problems and issues can be examined scientifically and successful strategies for solving them can be discovered. John Dewey found the support for this assumption and his naturalistic ethical theory in biological evolution. According to Dewey's ethical naturalism, moral and ethical judgments state a particular kind of fact about the natural world. In contrast to the commonly held view that statements about ethics and statements about nature are two entirely different classes of statements, ethical naturalism investigates and reports on morals and ethics as part of the same natural environs over which scientists have reigned since the eighteenth century.

For the ethical naturalist, decisions about the good or bad, and right or wrong are factual judgments; we may study them and trace their consequences in actual experience. While ethics and morals are not like physics or chemistry, which yield theories and laws, they are subject to similar sorts of investigatory techniques. Thus, while there may not be a science of ethics, it may be investigated scientifically and yield tentative or useful strategies and techniques for value resolution in the future.

Naturalistic Fallacy

G. E. Moore could not have disagreed more. In his book *Principia Ethica* (1903), Moore argued that good is a unique, unanalyzable, nonnatural property. You cannot see it, taste it, or hear it. Moore formulated the "naturalistic fallacy," or the view that trying to argue from a statement of fact to an ethical statement is wrong. Those people who seek to make a judgment about good or bad choices on the back of a claim about what is or is not true about a natural condition commit a logical error. Simply put, trying to argue from an "is" to an "ought" is a fallacy of a naturalistic kind, because it treats the two statements as if they are the same species of claim (and they are not).

The ethical naturalists fought back. For them, we are always considering descriptions and explanations of experience in making choices. Arguing from what we know about a situation to what we recommend doing about it is not a fallacy but a natural feature of human life. On the other hand, trying to locate the good, as an unanalyzed property of things is impossible. G. E. Moore never was able to demonstrate what this primal good is or why it has a bearing on our choices in the first place!

Natural Selection

The ethical naturalist took Charles Darwin more seriously than the rest of the moral philosophers. Darwin offered a solution to the problem of how evolution affects the choices of a species: the mechanism of "natural selection." When we apply natural selection to ethics we see that in any population of human beings there are inherited differences between individuals. Some individuals may be more guarded or less assertive, or possess more testosterone, for example, which affects their choices of courses of action. Testosterone has already been shown to produce highly physical reactions, and sometimes violence in people who take testosterone drugs, such as bodybuilders.

Next, natural selection tells us that heritable traits affect the ability of a person to survive. The ethical bearing of this feature of evolution has not been sufficiently tested. However, consider the case of a person born with a fatal disease that culminates in his death before the age of ten years. Since that child has not fully developed physically, we would not wish to say that he is responsible for making complex ethical choices regarding his own future. A child who tells the teacher he wishes to commit suicide would clearly be in the wrong for making the choice to end his own life.

We know from life insurance tables that not every person in a population will survive to old age. Some members of the population will survive longer, have more children, and be healthier than others. The notion of physical survival as a mechanism for natural selection affects a population of choosers. The longer an individual member of a group survives, the longer he or she may be involved in the activity of choosing. Choice and ethics work in tandem. For example, as people age, those who select survival-positive activities will have a greater propensity to continue to survive (and thus to make more choices). Ethics and survival work here to ensure that the individual continues to "play the game."

The more circumstances in which you may choose to live, the greater your impact for good or evil. The larger the population pool that will be affected, the greater the natural selectivity operates to ensure some ethical choices continue to dominate, while others do not. Consider the nineteenth century religious communities in the United States. Some selected the rule of chastity and forbade members to have sexual relations. These communities thus had to rely upon new recruits from outside the community to keep up their numbers. The normal natural selection of human reproduction could not enter the survivalist equation.

The more individuals there are who make certain kinds of moral and ethical decisions (as these relate to survival of their kind), the more opportunities there are to spread their philosophy of ethics and choice. A Malthusian phenomenon takes over and we find a branching and increase in fewer surviving choosers. For example, in a culture where graft and corruption emerge, it is more likely that these behaviors will continue than decline in numbers as the number of choosers adopt this kind of unethical behavior. The abundance of unethical and immoral behaviors, then, increases.

Traits of character and their application may increase or decrease in frequency. The frequency of decisions driven by character traits is tied to the evolution of the population in moral and ethical terms. For example, if honesty is celebrated and rewards are present in a culture for honest choices and acts, that trait will be attached to the survival of the members of the population. Here we may look at the statistics of prison populations in the United States. Certain acts are deemed both legally wrong and morally and ethically wrong (e.g., drug dealing). Choosing to be a drug dealer is thus not a survivalist option where laws against it are strongly enforced.

Finally, we need to think of fitness as a key component of evolution as it is applied to ethics. Fitness is the capacity of a group of persons to pass on the characteristics of moral and ethical thought and practice (good ethical and moral choices) to the young. Clearly, no human population lives forever. Certain individuals will die, and new individuals will be born. The group continues. However, unless the good-making moral and ethical characteristics of the choosers is taught, and learned by the younger members of the population, fitness (as measured by successful choices) will decline. When youth are unprepared for the culture and society of which they are members in terms of moral and ethical judging ability, the culture group will cease to be "fit."

Moral and Ethical Devolution

We must consider the case in which morals and ethics have eroded. Here, as with the case of physical disease, the population may suffer and die out. When members are no longer able to make the proper moral and ethical choices, their survival rate declines.

Moral and ethical devolution is not purely organic, but rather cognitive and emotional. Features of this disease are chaotic decision making, lack of understanding of the rules and standards of a group or population, and mistaken emphases.

Convergent, Divergent, and Parallel Evolution of Morality

The ethical and moral may be termed "convergent" in evolutionary terms when two different groups within a population come to possess similar structures. These may be organizational structures in education, and often are. For example, when two magnet school populations (teachers, students, parents of students, etc.) come together, they may well evolve into structures that share common components (e.g, interactions of parents and teachers, school board support, etc.).

Divergent evolution in moral and ethical spaces is defined by a branching of choices. Here, two kinds of schools (e.g., recently restructured middle schools versus traditional high schools) may pick quite different coping mechanisms to react to a relative lack of funds (e.g., parent-driven sales campaign versus teacher-driven austerity program). Divergent evolution results in a greater number of choices with quite different results.

Parallel evolution is evident historically in populations that select certain moral and ethical choice strategies, yet are not in communication with each other. We find common shibboleths against cannibalism, incest, and so on, in culture groups quite physically distant. These different groups may go through the same evolutionary changes due to similar selective pressures placed upon them by their environment. For example, lack of food may result in cannibalism. Certain individuals would survive as they adapted to the environs, and some would survive as they adjusted to the rule breaking they had to engage in to survive.

What Does Science Mean for Ethical School Leadership?

In all cases, human groups that seek to educate their young are fully invested in the culture and society of which they are members. The mechanisms that regulate such contexts are evolutionary. Natural selection, survival, fitness, and convergency work for perpetuation of the group or against it. Educational leaders who make choices need to realize that such choices are value decisions that may have a serious moral and ethical impact upon the group and its destiny.

Healthy (fit) schools seem to find individuals engaging in value choices that enhance their survival characteristics, while unhealthy ones do not. Studies of good schools point to inherent features of the school environment that promote survival. If schools are to do a better job with their students, it is essential that the teachers and parents, counselors and board members be well versed in moral and ethical decision making. Creating and sustaining good schools is not a crapshoot!

Conclusion

The foregoing recommends some general remarks concerning educational leadership, ethics, and human biological evolution. In light of what has been said here, it would seem that morality and moral education are best viewed as being within human biological evolutionary development, with the unique additive of human rationality shaping and being shaped by that development. As Bergson pointed out, there do seem to be two sources of ethics: society and the individual. Both sources are found within the scope of reason. In short, we may derive a morality from socially dictated obligation, which is in no sense irrational, as well as finding, through the use of intelligence, the capacity to reconstruct moral ideas to guide human action.

We do not need to get our moral ideals from mysticism or religious revelation, as Bergson argued (Bidney, 1967). Reflective thinking itself may be a source of dispositions toward ethical behavior, as Kant asserts, and such thinking may provide us with ethical ideals toward which to strive. However, the notion that there can be a supremacy of such abstract reason is not without its shortcomings. Increasingly, we have seen human rationality questioned by contemporary theorists.

Henri Bergson seems to shortchange the role of such reason in determining moral obligations and aspirations. In this, Bergson is closer to postmodernists and poststructuralists. On the other hand, reducing morality to the level of emotion, as Westermarck does, seems to produce a kind of ethical subjectivity that has no portability in current terms. Nor is it reasonable to hold with Nietzsche that ethics are relative to social class. Such an approach precludes the possibility of judging the worth of moral codes viewed cross-culturally without being labeled ethnocentric.

It would seem that ethics is both a means and an end. Ethics is a means as it is social, while it is an end in itself as it is individual. While most ethnologists are concerned with ethics as means, they ought to attend to ethics as an end, as Bergson does. Ethics may be a pragmatic moral ideal.

Ethics is relative in the sense that it is a means and subserves the biological evolutionary end of self-preservation. Further, ethics is relative to humans in the sense that any moral code that is counter to human biological ends will eliminate itself. There is a paradox in morality: ethics must be relative biologically as it is in harmony and conformity with the requirements of human species-specific survival; however, ethics superimposes an ideal beyond self-preservation that may call for the sacrifice of life for the common good of the group. In short, all morality and moral education must be limited by natural laws of cosmic nature, but must be emancipatory as it seeks to improve the conditions of mankind.

Schooling provides a means whereby the ethics of evolution may be studied in the effort to provide an evolutionary ethics (one that transcends the limits imposed by historic conditions). The breakthroughs in genetic engineering, mechanical implants, and organ transplants have opened the range of moral choices, shifted and enlarged the ethical issues facing human beings. Given the scientific breakthroughs, it would be reasonable to attempt to teach children the evolutionary fact that the biological evolutionary bases for morals and ethics are changing and that societal and cultural value conditions are being transformed as well. We cannot teach naive "survival" when the biological conditions that define such survival of the fittest are undergoing radical reconstruction.

Finally, reflective thought may be a guide, but not in its unadulterated form. The scientific bases for ethics are themselves shifting and changing as the social and cultural drama plays out. The morality of the twenty-first century will be as much a product of the biological changes brought on by new technologies as will be the perception of such morality. If evolution is a fact, then it is a fact everywhere. Evolution must be taken seriously if we are to meet the challenges facing our children now and in the future.

8

Practical Ethics Strategies

"Just as physical life cannot exist without the
support of a physical environment, so moral life cannot go on
without the support of a moral environment."
— John Dewey, *Art as Experience*

Administration Ethics versus Leadership Ethics

Those moral and ethical dilemmas that occur within the broad area of administration tend to deal with management, supervision, or the direction of some group or set of activities. The prime responsibility of administrators is to oversee the work to be done. Matters of appropriateness of mission, degree of dedication, trust, honesty, and so forth do not appear to be central. Hence, administration, although subject to ethical considerations, is for the most part procedural and technical in nature.

Leadership is different. Here the aim is not so much to maintain things as they are (although some maintenance may be called for), but rather to move the group toward some goal(s). Leadership is all about values. Ethics as it relates to leadership is more focused upon the determination of the good toward which the group is working and the selection of proper means for the achievement of that end. The arena here is qualitative, or value laden. Since the goal is riddled with values, it is not surprising that we may find the day-to-day relational dealings among people to be filled with moral and ethical dilemmas.

For example, recall the Case of the Lonely Bureaucrat. Mrs. X received a grant to do a special project of educational work in her school system. She hired several teachers to help and told them they had to "kick back" a certain percentage of their salaries to Mrs. X because she had hired them. News leaked out, and Mrs. X was notified by the head to come in and talk. She lost her job. Before long the case was in court.

Administration that is cut and dried may not be so subject to ethical difficulties. The fact that Mrs. X received the grant and yet sought to make herself even wealthier caused her eventual fall. She had perhaps read of former governor of Louisiana, Huey Long, and his "Deduct Box"—a device used to milk kickback money from political job holders. Illegal and unethical, this practice found Long murdered and the Box missing! Leadership seems to have more difficulty with ethics than bureaucracy, perhaps because it allows more freedom to make mistakes.

Considerations Going into Ethical Decisions

Ethics is practical when it seeks to deal with certain issues of teaching, counseling, coaching, or other practices within the contested space called "school," using one's wisdom and decision-making skills. A leader needs to consider a number of anticipatory dispositions at the beginning of the moral and ethical decision-making process.

Problem and Issues Oriented

Are you looking for the moral and ethical elements in the problems and issues you face? If it is not characteristically a moral and ethical dilemma, then forget about using a moral and ethical analysis approach to it. For example, if the district judge tells you that you must either use the temporary buildings on your school site or send so many children to another school, your choice is procedural (fill them with students or have them hauled away). You are not making a moral and ethical choice here. Acts like preparing the coffee for the faculty meeting, turning in attendance reports, scheduling buses, and so forth are just part of your day-to-day performance as a school administrator. However, if the decision calls for you to consider your own and the other person's values, or the values of the school and society, you are within the moral and ethical domain.

Open-Minded

It is vital to keep an open mind. The consideration of facts and personal opinions means that you are taking in matters you may not agree with. Nevertheless, it is important to consider all sides in an argument and to entertain the possibility that you may not be correct.

Free to Choose

Unless you are free to make a decision, you cannot resolve a moral and ethical dilemma, nor may you be held responsible. If your superintendent phones you and tells you not to suspend a student who has been caught with a gun, you are bound by his direction. You are not responsible for the choice. You are not free to choose in this situation.

However, if you are free to choose and there are at least two options you may pick from, and if the problem or issue is a moral and ethical one, then your choice will be morally or ethically correct or not. You are free and you are thus responsible for your decision.

Aware of Relevant Laws, Policies, and Rules

Ethics often involves rules, principles, and standards. At a young age we learn moral rules such as "do not tell a lie." Yet simple rules are just that— simple. As we mature, we come to realize that rules do not apply evenly to every moral and ethical dilemma we face. Sometimes it is difficult to apply them at all in tough cases. We must consider rules, principles, and standards but realize that they are rough guidelines, benchmarks, and rubrics that are tested in time and rebuilt with each decision we make. We should recall the example of the teacher who was convinced that "honesty is the best policy." When accosted by a thief on a darken street and asked, "Where is your money?" as a truthful person, she told him!

Ethics also involves concrete goals and ends. However, much harm has been done by people slipping into the simple acceptance that "the end justifies the means." Administrators have been faulted for never questioning the aims and goals set for them by their superiors. During World War II SS Lieutenant-Colonel Adolf Eichmann (1906–1962) was a model of bureaucratic industriousness and clear determination. Placed in charge of death camp operations, he sought to speed Adolf Hitler's "Final Solution" toward its end by murdering hundreds of thousands of Jews. He was highly effective and efficient at filling the Nazi death camps with Jewish prisoners, processing them, and signing the certificates placing each person in the gas chamber. Good administrator that he was, he complained that there were too many obstacles to his meeting the standard set by the Nazis. He had difficulty carrying out his job. At his trial in Israel after the war, he claimed he was innocent and just followed orders!

Standards, rules, and principles themselves need to be tested. A standard may be judged as worthwhile or not based on how well it fulfills the image or vision of the good school, good teaching and learning, good community, or good society. A standard is measured relative to Quality. It can also be tested in another way by asking what the standard does for directing the course of human action as revealed by its practical results.

For example, a standard governing field trips that called for 85 to 95 percent success would be efficient and effective on the number side alone, but the school leader who drove off and left one or two students behind at the museum or historic site would not be ethical. We would say the standard is a poor one and in need of revision, given the impact on the quality of school life and on the individual children left at the museum!

Down-to-Earth

Being practical in ethics also means that our ethics will be down-to-earth, without frills, and operative beyond the borders of local or national law. A practical ethicist is one who works with the essentials of a dilemma marked by value differences and has no pretensions about who she is or what constitutes her authority on ethical matters. She wishes to see tangible results come to the school and the individuals involved. She hopes the experience and choice will add positively to the sum total of her own moral character as well as to the moral character of the members of the school.

By way of example, a principal asked a few fellow administrators if she had done the right thing. One of the teachers in her school would not stay in her classroom. At every opportunity she moved into the hall to talk with other teachers or simply to get away from her students. The principal, sensitive to the absence of the teacher from the classroom, warned her several times that she "needed to stay with her children." No change in behavior occurred. She threw up her hands and said, "What am I to do—she will not listen to me! Should I create a policy or rule calling for each teacher to stay in her classroom while the students are there? Should I call the superintendent and report this teacher's behavior?"

Another principal in the group advised her this way: "You are trying to make another rule? The teachers have enough rules! You really need to show her why it is not ethically right for her to be out of her classroom so much. A confrontation is not necessary. If you were to tell her that she is not being professional she might change her ways. If you were to tell her that if she is not in the classroom and some child were to have an accident or come to harm, she would be responsible. The damages could be dangerous, life threatening, or expensive. Or, if you were to tell all teachers in your monthly faculty meeting that evaluations of teaching will be more sensitive to the ethical responsibilities of teaching. Well, then she might get the message."

Keeping It Simple

The English philosopher William of Ockham (1285–1349) invented what would be called "Ockham's Razor," or the maxim that when confronted with two competing theories aimed at explaining the same thing, the simpler is better.

The Ockhamist school leader of today believes the solution to a moral and ethical dilemma is best when it (1) relies upon scientific investigation into the case, (2) is disentangled from the arcane logic games, and (3) is rendered in the simplest practical terms in the shortest time possible.

School leaders do not have a lot of extra time. We need to know if the decision can be made in a timely manner or will be interrupted. Will I have to put this decision "on the back burner," because something else is more important? By keeping the decision-making process as simple as possible, you may be able to make the decision and get on with other matters.

Bias Free

There is a great difference between someone's personal religion and his or her ethics. Ethics is not about religion, private faith, or deeply held religious beliefs. Although for centuries, ethical beliefs and religious beliefs were found in religious texts and fought about in wars, science has shown that ethical and religious values need not be the same. Recall Bayle's argument that an atheist may be moral, and a devoted Christian can be immoral. Singer (1979) points out that we need to separate out ethics from theological talk and practice.

Consider the following: A school principal decides, based upon his faith (Islam) that all women in the school should stand in the hallway during faculty meetings. Another school leader (Quaker) asks the social studies teacher to refrain from teaching about war in his fourth-hour class. And yet another school leader (atheist) tells the football coach that prayers in the locker room before the games will not be allowed. In each of these cases, the merits of the issue are set in bold relief through the importation of a belief that is tied to a religious orientation.

Public school spaces are not arenas for the exercise of our private religious beliefs.

Beyond the Absolute and the Relative

We must be on guard against absolutists and relativists in ethical decision making. They may well tell us, "You must decide in this way because it is the only right thing to do!" To believe in a moral and ethical absolute is simple-minded and lazy. Only hard thinking and weighing of data and evidence can aid us here. Each moral and ethical dilemma is different, if not in kind, in details. We are not the same person, nor is our school the same as it was the last time this ethical issue came across our desk.

The relativist tells us: "Ethics is relative. There is no right or wrong. When in Rome, do as the Romans do!" This abject relativism removes responsibility for the decision from the leader. If every ethical decision is relative, then why do we wrestle with standards, rules, and principles in making our choices? Why do we consider the context and test our choices against their practical impact upon people?

Ethics is not purely relative, nor is it completely absolute. Ethics is beyond absolutism and relativism in the sense that ethical standards and norms are changing, ethical leaders change, and the context in which decisions are made changes.

Scientific and Artistic

To be an expert ethical leader requires that a person develop a repertoire of strategies and skills, rooted in wise scholarship and honed by extensive repetitive practice. The attitude is one of the scientist, without the assurance that a body of scientific facts await our use. This so-called scientific approach differs from scientific method as a formal set of procedures that are followed in unswerving ways.

We are, each time we exercise a moral and ethical choice, interpreting a particular instance against our common sense, rules, and results. All of these are changing so that our imagination and dramatic rehearsal are creatively called upon in making sound ethical decisions.

Doing Ethics: A Strategy for Ethical Decision Making

The preceding chapters have addressed the understanding of the place of ethics in leadership and the school. We have explored the foundations of ethical thinking and leading with a moral and ethical eye. What we shall do now is provide a schematic for actually doing ethics in a practical and meaningful way. Even though a step-by-step procedure is outlined, by no means are you to be held to this order or arrangement of concerns. It is possible to follow key ideas but move about within the structure outlined here, selecting appropriate actions.

Ethical naturalism, of all the schools of ethics, seems to provide a method for doing ethics in the best practical and meaningful way. In the following pages we will subscribe to this approach to ethics because it seems to solve so many of the problems people have had with doing ethics.

Essentially, this naturalistic view of ethical decision making argues that the value of any moral and ethical decision is to be judged in terms of how well the choice reconstructs or reorders the problem situation. If it reconstructs it well, then new decisions are no longer a difficulty or barrier to the flow of experience. Naturalists indicate that doing leadership ethics includes the following general ideas:

1. *Morals and Ethics and Ordinary Experience.* A moral and ethical dilemma is a normal situation in life that finds a conflict between two or more interests, desires, or needs; it impacts you or other persons in terms of human character and future conduct in both one's professional career and as a fuller way of living.

2. *Quality.* The question of Quality must be faced when the educational leadership decision affects or influences the social space of the school where people live and work, learn and teach.

3. *Standards.* A standard, rule, or principle offers a meaningful device for understanding our experience (teaching, coaching, counseling, etc.) such that it may lead to or cause human performances to fulfill certain needs, interests, or desires.

4. *Consequences.* Choosing or deciding between conflicting needs, interests, and desires is aided when the standard helps us to understand whether option A delivers better results relative to these needs, desires, and interests than option B.

What Do I Have to Work With?

We all have our experiences and prior learnings regarding moral and ethical quandaries and decision making. These precedents help us in a new situation to resolve ethical discord and disagreement. We also have the standards, rules, policies, laws, and principles that are operative in a space like a school. We know something about human behavior and the boundaries surrounding action. And we have the inquiry or investigation skills (practical intelligence) acquired from experience and education that help us burrow into conflicts to lift out the competing value positions that exist in the situation.

Judgment and Quality

We have discussed the origin of moral and ethical quandaries in the realm of Quality. Judgments of right and wrong, good or bad are dealt with through the lens of quality, and therefore qualitative judgments are called for. Some ethical theories and reasoning schemes are remote and impractical for the everyday world of communities like schools.

Practical Intelligence

What is often called "common sense" might better be phrased "practical intelligence." This kind of thoughtful or critical mind can be compared to the investigatory techniques of Sherlock Holmes, or the logical strategies of Popeye. Down-to-earth, no-nonsense, and getting right to the heart of the issue is what this kind of burrowing is all about.

It is practical, too, in that it aims at making decisions that make a difference in practice, in the ways we do things. Theoretical intelligence is important, but within emotionally charged schools, a practical mentality is often better than a deep philosophical one.

Value Sensitivity

Often ethical dilemmas are matters of conflicting values. The individual student may have a set of values that comes into conflict with the school. For example, the dress code may required that boys must keep their shirts tucked into their pants, or girls may not wear short-shorts to school. Such rules can come into conflict with a child's own desire to dress the way he or she wishes by leaving his shirt out or wearing short-shorts.

The individual may come into conflict with another person's values. Playground ethical dilemmas are often student-on-student disagreements about something each holds dear. The bully wishes to punch the smaller child; his need for the feeling of power over others comes into conflict with the smaller child's desire for safety and security.

The individual's values may come into conflict with a set of values that has its origin in the community, and that the school valorizes. For example, a teacher may be of a particular faith that has strict dietary rules. The athletic banquet may offer only the foods the teacher is forbidden to eat. She complains. As a principal, you may wish to become sensitive to her dietary rules and pass on this information to the kitchen staff so that something she can eat is served (thus eliminating further conflict and resolving her problem); or you can tell her she does not have to eat (thus creating further difficulties and failing to resolve the problem).

There may be a conflict between an individual's values and those of the culture. For example, a teacher may be hired on the premise that he will teach physical education classes. The principal may receive reports that he is teaching sexual promiscuity under the banner of "free love." He declares HIV a myth and he invites students to view videos that are rated X. A culture's values and the individual's values are in conflict and the results may lead to serious problems for the teacher, the school, the community, and its culture.

Creativity and Visualization

One of the most powerful tools you may use in making good moral and ethical decisions is visualization. Picturing in your mind the actual impacts of the moral and ethical decision is one of the best ways to weigh the good-making or bad-making consequences of your choice. For example, if you must choose between two students to receive a scholarship, it is helpful to picture in your mind's eye what they may be doing in the next school semester. Will they be attending a college, or will you see them behind the counter at the Big Burger? If you fail to pick the other student, do you "see" him or her in college anyway?

Picturing the concrete outcomes of moral and ethical choices, with practice, results in the logical extrapolation of a decision to the concrete consequences in the everyday world. Try to picture yourself in the student's place. What will life be like if this choice favors this person over the other?

You may even "walk your way through" the events that will follow on the heels of your choice. Step by step you may see the good or bad things that can happen to the student. We call this visualization a dramatic rehearsal. John Dewey first popularized this technique as a way of evaluating a value.

A Conception of School as Space and an Understanding of Moral Character

All of the above leads us to conclude that the core virtue of our practical ethics is a reliance upon the capacity of an individual to engage in practical thinking—with an eye to communicating with others, looking to commonalities, and seeing the kind of community involved—as necessary to judge what ought to be done in an ethical dilemma. Some political scientists claim that only a select few intellectuals know what is best for the rest of us. They caution us not to employ democratic processes in elementary or secondary schools because such places are not populated by experts. Pragmatists believe that informed judgment is a natural consequence of allowing the freedom to inquire to spread. Coupled with the sharing of findings, this democratic approach will result in a greater sharing of the leadership in our institutions.

Understanding the context is only half of it. You also must understand yourself. It is crucial that you have a values pivot point or core moral and ethical character to which you may appeal in making moral and ethical decisions. This moral character, as we have seen, is developed as we mature and refined through intelligence and choice. As a school leader, your ethical decisions are observed by others within the school—students, teachers, and staff. Your decisions affect these individuals and the school as a whole. The success or failure of the moral space of the school is affected by your moral and ethical leadership.

A Well-Defined Conception of Leadership

Typically, a leadership philosophy that will work must consider the following:

1. *Communication Skills.* Where we see schools, the community, and our culture as democratic spaces, we naturally gravitate toward using the tools of democracy in our practical activities. Through communicating the results of

inquiries, it is possible to select superior alternative paths to more successful practice.

2. *Commonality.* Recognizing the things we hold in common may be the basis for ameliorating differences. Look to the case to see what the contesting parties may agree on, not just disagree over.

3. *Community.* New school spaces that are more democratic in nature may result from using practical thinking to resolve ethical difficulties. A critical and practical ethics flourishes within this space as a democratic context, for democracy both enables the criticism of school practices, and allows for the fuller publication of the results of such inquiries.

4. *Good-Making and Bad-Making Features of Choice.* Once committed to a choice in a moral and ethical dilemma, it is wise to investigate whether the choice will yield good or bad results. A moral and ethical choice not only makes a decision or selection between alternatives: we may further ask if the alternative chosen reflects back upon this particular choice in similar cases with any worth or value. For example, if you decide to send a fifth grader home for threatening a seventh grader who has been taunting him, you need to realize that bullying may be reinforced and reports of harassment lessened in the future.

5. *Good-Making and Bad-Making Features of Standards.* We have discovered that the good-making features of a choice may bring to fruit the value of a standard, principle, or rule. Thus, if the choice is proper and quiets concern and doubt about what is to be done, it may also tell us something about the value of the standard, principle, or rule used in making the decision. For example, let us say a school board member decides to vote for a new school to be built in the community because she believes that the "best educated children will result from the best educational facility." The standard of measure is given a hallowed or good-making status as part of this choice. The standard could later be employed in a vote regarding something like enlarging the library.

Educators are often encouraged to be satisified with mere efficiency or effectiveness, rather than explore and actively reveal the ethical values that support our institutional lives. Deontologists, we have learned, believe standards or norms of practice are set out by professional organizations to act as guides for practicing educators. A practical ethics that is artistic should explore these standards and norms with an eye to creatively building upon them. This can be difficult, for we take for granted the status of institutional values of schooling as unassailable rubrics for practice.

6. *Able to Make a Decision and Learn from It.* Another way in which we may find good-making attached to a choice is through the inspection of its results. For example, if the same school board member voted against the new school because she believed that building the school would put the district seriously in debt, then the standard (money) takes on power where financial insolvency would dictate the choice.

7. *Willing to Stay Around to Check the Results.* It is important for us to examine the likely practical consequences resulting from our ethical leadership decision for the school. We have seen that teleologists, like the utilitarians are concerned with the bottom-line effects of a moral and ethical decision. Too often the skills of management and administration of schooling stop short of this, asking only if the goal has been achieved. But a really practical and ethical concern for leading a classroom, school, or school system must always consider the possible moral and ethical consequences of every decision for the people involved or likely to become involved.

8. *Ethical Leadership as a Professional Approach and a Fuller Way of Living.* Under this consideration we are interested in two matters: (1) What is the decision about? and (2) How does the dilemma and decision fit into the larger way of living manifested in the institution? If a school is dedicated to preparing students for jobs in the oil refineries in the community, we may say that this larger way of living as a refinery worker bears on the decision. If the goal of the school is to send its students to college, then the way of living is connected to intellectual and institutional values. Here the decision may reflect codes of conduct for the educated and educator alike.

How well or poorly the leader devises the ethical decision is a reflection of his or her implicit view of moral and ethical leadership. Hodgkinson (1991) puts it well when he says, "the quality of leadership is functionally related to the moral climate of the organization and this, in turn, to the moral complexity and skills of the leader" (p. 129). This view needs to be expanded, however. The quality of morals-ethics exists not only in the space and climate of an institution, and the leader, but in the ways in which conditions, human participants, and school community members transact the business of learning and growing. It is the responsibility of leadership to use intelligence and inquiry, cooperatively and collaboratively, to arrive at moral judgments in terms of the individual's and the group's needs, desires, and interests, but also relative to the moral and ethical parts of the school mission. Without variation, schools are dedicated to the goal of teaching and learning. Thus, our definition of leadership as ethical must include these considerations of the modes of inquiry and the values operating within the school settings. With the experience of using moral and ethical tools, leadership may be fused with values to result in an ongoing engagement with Quality.

The Steps of Analysis

In table 8.1, you will find laid out the step-by-step process that may be used to deal with a moral and ethical problem or issue.

Table 8. 1 Schema for Practical Ethical Decision Making

Step 1. Gain Knowledge and Understanding
    A. Interview Affected Parties
    B. Read Related Documents
    C. Collect Material Evidence
    D. Determine Relevant Policies

Step 2. Identify Elements of the Issue
    A. Determine Problem Area and Issue
    B. Find Conflicting Points of View
Step 3. Reflect
    A. Determine Personal Moral and Ethical Position and Leadership Style
    Moral and Ethical Position
        1. Traditionalism
        2. Realism
        3. Idealism
        4. Utilitarianism
        5. Emotivism
        6. Subjectivism
        7. Existentialism
        8. Naturalism
    Leadership Style
        1. Charismatic
        2. Bureaucratic
        3. Servant
        4. Transformational or Radical
        5. Reflective

Table 8. 1 Schema for Practical Ethical Decision-Making *(continued)*

    B. Select Appropriate Dispositions and Attitudes
        1. Just and Fair
        2. Caring
        3. Rights-Sensitive
        4. Common Good
        5. Least Harm
        6. Courage
        7. Temperance
        8. Prudence
        9. Honesty
    C. Lay Out Options
    D. Trace Likely Consequences of Each Options

Step 4. Make Decision

Step 5. Live with Decision and Learn from It

Step 1. Gain Knowledge and Understanding

A. Interview Affected Parties. Once a moral and ethical dilemma is apparent, it is important to gather as much information as possible about what took place. Interviews of the students, teachers, parents, or others who were involved or witnessed the events should be conducted. Make a file and keep careful notes of what you learn.

For example, when the principal of Centerville High School, Bill Hanson, heard from the Prom Committee chairperson, student Donna Henderson, that the decorations for the dance were missing from the gym, he decided to speak to the committee members.

B. Read Related Documents. It is not unusual for there to be a "paper trail" or "electronic trail" in a case of moral or ethical difficulty. Find these pieces of information and read them. If there are memoranda, e-mails, or notes, make copies for the file. Create a time line in which these documents were created, received, or used.

Principal Hanson continued his investigation by checking the waste baskets in the gym, where he found several notes from Donna Henderson about a particular band she wished to use for the dance.

C. Collect Material Evidence. If a torn shirt, broken charm bracelet, or any other item involved in the case is relevant, tag it and place it in a safe place. The authorities may ask for this if the case goes to court.

In one of the football players' lockers, Mr. Hanson discovered a bag of balloons, which Donna Henderson later told him were like those her committee had purchased. Mr. Hanson called the team member, Chad Elliot, into his office the next morning. Chad, quarterback on the team, confessed to convincing two other football team members to help him move the decorations to the storage building next to the stadium.

D. *Determine Relevant Policies.* What laws, policies, or rules are relevant in this case? Find these regulating statements and make copies. Jot down how the case fits under the law, policy, or rule and whether it is federal, state, local, school district, or school based. Keep all of this information in the file.

In our example, Principal Hanson checked the Centerville School District policy statements on stealing school property and discovered that the rule was quite specific. If the thief were located and the evidence secured, the principal should contact local police authorities.

Step 2. Identify Elements of the Issue

A. *Determine Problem Area and Issue.* Most dilemmas are half solved after they have been classified as a certain kind of problem and issue. Following up with our example, Mr. Hanson wondered what problem area and issue he was dealing with here. If it was a matter of the three football players having taken the prom decorations, it was theft. Because these decorations were created by the students using school funds, this was a theft from the school. The problem area would probably be academic dishonesty. Mr. Hanson recalled another case he had handled in which a student had stolen another student's term paper and turned it in as his own.

There are a number of large problem areas in education. His Foundations of Education classes at the university had dealt with such problems as equal educational opportunity, church-state and education, sexual harassment, and race, class, gender, and ethnicity problem areas, he recalled. The fascinating cases in the course called for him to really think deeply and discuss his ideas with other students.

Mr. Hanson thought about each of these problem areas and concluded that the present case fit into the area of academic dishonesty.

B. *Find Conflicting Points of View.* Conflicts and dilemmas are part of every school leader's experiences, Mr. Hanson believed. To have a contested issue, all that you need are at least two sides to the controversy.

When he spoke with the football players, they broke down and said that the prom was not representative of what the students wanted. The band that Donna Henderson wanted to hire was terrible. As a matter of protest, they thought it was okay for them to steal the prom decorations. Donna Henderson argued that stealing the decorations was wrong, since the committee had been elected by the student body as their representatives to put on the dance.

Hanson concluded that this problem really had two issues attached to it. First, the incident involving the stealing of the prom decorations, and second the controversial issue about which band should play at the prom and how that had been decided. Donna Henderson claimed she and her committee were hurt when they were deprived of the decorations needed for the prom. The three football players argued that they only "borrowed" the decorations to illustrate the point that Donna had chosen a band without any student (or committee) input, and the band leader was her cousin! This was so selfish, the players contended, that they had to disobey the rules and take the decorations.

Step 3. Reflect

A. Determine Personal Moral and Ethical Position and Leadership Style. We learned earlier that a number of moral and ethical philosophies have been handed down through time: traditionalism, realism, idealism, utilitarianism, emotivism, subjectivism, existentialism, and naturalism. Select the moral and ethical position most representative of your personal philosophy and consider how it informs the decision you must make in the case.

Principal Bill Hanson believed naturalism was the best moral and ethical approach to follow. It allowed him to dig deeply into the evidence and to think through the case as if he were wrestling with a personal ethical dilemma.

Next, consider your leadership style. What model of leadership do you embrace? Which model do you emulate: charismatic, bureaucratic, servant, transformational or radical, or reflective leadership? How does your leadership approach fit the conditions of the case you are addressing?

Principal Hanson was a reflective leader. He thought deeply about things and liked to listen to other options before he made his decision.

B. Select Appropriate Dispositions or Attitudes. Here it is important to determine which dispositions or attitudes you shall take relative to the case at hand. In this case of the stolen prom decorations, Principal Hanson felt he must go into this with a just and fair attitude. Whatever emerged, the treatment of students involved had to be balanced, with an eye to the good of the school. He also felt he should be caring. After all, these were adolescents and their moral character was still in the formation stage. He felt compassion for them all. Nor did he wish to harm anyone involved in this case. As seniors, they would be gone soon. College offered new contexts and opportunities. The students ought not to have to carry these negative experiences into their next steps in education.

If he was just and fair, he would select the appropriate policy of the school district and use it to determine the punishment for the students involved. But Bill Hanson had a great deal of experience as an assistant principal and knew that a caring attitude might work better in this case. He therefore looked at the students who pulled the prank as misguided and not criminals.

C. Lay Out Options. A true dilemma offers two or more openings for resolution. Of course your first inclination will probably be to flee as far as possible from the problem, but that is your emotional self kicking in. Once resigned to the fact that you must make a decision, sort out the choices that make the most sense to you.

Try to attach the best reasons you can think of to each of the choices set out. You may want to use the interview materials you have in your file. Argue them persuasively on paper, being honest about each option.

If several options are available, a table with rows and columns may come in handy for arranging the options and rationales for each.

In the present case, Principal Hanson could either forgive the boys for their prank after they agreed to restore the decorations to the gym, or he could punish them in some way for stealing the school's property. However, the issue concerning the band and how it was selected had a bearing on this decision. He needed to get this cleared up as well.

D. Trace Likely Consequences of Each Option. For each option trace the likely consequences. If you chose option A, how will it affect the individuals involved? How will this choice affect the good of the school?

There may be intended consequences on your chart. But do not overlook unintended consequences of each choice. Often these are the results that haunt you as a leader after you have made your decision.

If he punished the boys for stealing the decorations, he still would not have solved the problem of the band. Principal Hanson thought that by deciding against the boys, the original problem pretty much was left the way it was— unsettled. On the other hand, if he shifted to the issue of the band and Donna Henderson's undemocratic method of choosing it, he might make the students happier.

Step 4. Make Decision

Decide among the options which one is the best, for the reasons outlined. Make the decision. Contact all the involved individuals regarding your decision. It is often a good idea to call the affected persons into your office and talk to each, one at a time.

Bill Hanson decided to call Donna into his office and confront her with the band selection methods she used. She was not happy to be on the defensive after reporting the theft of the prom decorations, but she admitted that she alone chose her cousin Vincent Lobardo instead of the more popular group Rockin Dropsie. Bill Hanson explained that the students (football team) were protesting and did not mean to keep the decorations. They just wanted a more democratic means to be used in picking a band. Donna agreed that it was wrong for her to pick her cousin. She apologized. Bill Hanson then informed her that her insensitivity to the interests of the student body required that she learn a lesson. She was to be assigned to an after-school Service Learning project in the Deaf School nearby for a week.

Next, Bill Hanson called in the three football players. He said that their experiment in civil disobedience, while understandable, still broke the rules. He explained that it was wrong to take the prom decorations and that they had violated school policy. It was also wrong from a moral and ethical point of view, because stealing deprives people of things that are theirs and advantages the thieves at the expense of the victim. The three athletes agreed and said they were sorry. Bill then told the students that because they broke a rule, they would have to be punished. Their punishment, he told them, was to move all the decorations back into the gym and to assist Donna Henderson and the committee in decorating the gym for the dance that Saturday.

Then Bill admitted it was wrong for Donna Henderson to pick the band of her choice and not the band the students wanted. He told them he had punished her by assigning her to an after-school Service Learning project in the Deaf School for one week. She was to extend an official contract to Rockin Dropsie, the band the students wanted to play at the prom. The arrangement with the Vincent Lobardo band was to be canceled.

Step 5. Live with Decision and Learn from It

Bill Hanson was prepared to live with his decision. To punish the three football players for the prank, when he knew the motive for their hiding the decorations, would have been an overreaction. He knew that in the future, students would use more public and democratic means to select a band for the prom.

Writing Up the Case

As we have indicated, it is often a good idea to take notes when you are investigating a case and to write it up for the record. Using good grammar and a reasoned analysis, write up the case following the steps in table 8.1. Pay attention to the proper steps the administrator or teacher should take in such a case. Provide a thoughtful and logical analysis of why these procedures count in this particular way in the case at hand. If local policy, federal or state law, or other norm, rule, or standard is involved, mention this. Recall that leaders can make good legal decisions that are unethical. Pay attention to your own views and biases, keeping your analysis free from them as much as possible.

Conclude your analysis with a choice. Take a stance or position that illuminates the particulars of the case and shows how your practical decision (ethical and moral) could be made.

Earlier we pointed out that a natural, reflective, and practical approach to ethics is not necessarily a lockstep method. In appendix A for the sake of simplicity, we will lay out a sample case and moral and ethical decision-making strategy in steps. Keep in mind that steps may be skipped, returned to later, or ignored completely.

Conclusion

The scheme set forth in this chapter for making good moral and ethical decisions may be used for settling actual moral and ethical dilemmas in the schools. The appendixes to follow present cases on which you may practice and improve your skills of investigation, analysis, and decision making.

Appendix A

The Case of the Phony Resume

The following case deals with a new high school principal, a Mr. Wolf, who submits and has on file in the school district office a resume that indicates he has received a Ph.D. degree. After a normal review of all new principals' resumes, the office secretary alerts Dr. Howard Short, superintendent of schools, of a resume problem. Howard senses a moral and ethical dilemma and begins his investigation.

Mrs. Virginia Smiley, secretary to Dr. Howard Short, superintendent of District 812 Schools, seemed to take delight in thrusting the piece of paper across his desk. She had worked for Short for five years, and for a string of previous superintendents for over twenty-five years. Dr. Short glanced at the clock tower on the letterhead, then read the letter slowly.

Dear Mrs. Smiley:
We wish to respond to your inquiry regarding Mr. Stephen Wolf, now in employ of District 812. Mr. Wolf has been a graduate student at State University. He is not currently a student. Our records indicate he was last enrolled in the Ph.D. program in Educational Leadership two summers ago. Mr. Wolf passed his general examinations, but he has not completed the dissertation. In fact, as of this enrollment date he had neither formed a dissertation committee nor submitted a dissertation prospectus. The degree of Ph.D. certainly has not been awarded to Mr. Wolf by this institution.

Sincerely,

Roland Smart, Ph.D.
Dean of the Graduate School

Mrs. Smiley interjected, "Superintendent Short, I was doing a routine background check of all the resumes of our school principals when it occurred to me that no one had checked Dr. Wolf's credentials when he was hired two years ago. I contacted State University, the school he lists in his credentials as granting him the Ph.D . . ." Her voice trailed off into a whisper.

Howard Short swung his chair aggressively to face the wall. He spoke in short staccato phrases to the bookshelves. "This is a problem! . . . need to bring this before the School Board. . . . They are meeting weekend after next at my camp on the Ticktack River for a retreat. You've taken care of refreshments, haven't you? . . . never mind, increase the amount of food and drink . . . enough for five parents. Yes, I want you to invite the usual ones. . . . We need to talk. . . . Got to get a consensus on what to do about Wolf's outright lying on his resume!

"Mrs. Smiley, contact Mr. Wolf and ask him to come and see me when he gets the opportunity. I believe we need to get his side of this story." (Dr. Short had, after considering the gravity of the issue, decided to gather Mr. Wolf's view on the matter at hand.)

"Oh, and please get Dean Roland Smart on the phone, Mrs. Smiley. I want to speak to him about this letter."

Dr. Short's phone call to graduate school Dean Smart revealed that the Mr. Wolf who was enrolled in State's doctoral program in educational leadership several years prior was indeed the same Mr. Wolf who was currently acting as principal of Clinton High School. Dean Smart said, "Fire him!"

Dr. Short's interview with Mr. Wolf was short and to the point.

"Stephen, in doing a background search on our District 812 principals, your resume appeared to have some inconsistencies. You report in the resume you provided that you had received the Ph.D. from State U. However, I spoke with Dean Smart of the State U. Graduate School, and he verified that while you did attend State a few years ago, you were not granted the Ph.D. degree. Can you explain?

"Gee, Dr. Short, I was a graduate student in Ed Leadership at State and was working on my doctorate when I applied for the principal's job with the district. I didn't put a date next to the resume reference to the Ph.D. because I was working on it at the time. I kinda assumed people would understand this."

"Well, you allowed me, the teachers, and students at your school to call you 'doctor.' Wasn't that misleading?" Dr. Short interjected.

Stephen stood up. "Heck, the kids started calling me 'doc' and the teachers started to as well. I never bothered to correct people. It is difficult to explain how the university works. You can be working on a degree like this for a long time. I was an ABD (all but dissertation)."

"I certainly understand that a mistaken perception could have happened, but according to the Graduate School, you were not enrolled in the Ph.D. program at State when you joined our staff. If you were not actively taking classes or working on your dissertation, how could you interpret this as 'working toward the degree' when you took the job with us?"

Stephen Wolf scratched his head. "I needed a break. I didn't try to lie on my resume. It's just a misunderstanding, that's all. I'm doing a great job at the high school. Please don't tell anyone. I need this job."

Stephen Wolf put his head down, turned, and walked out of Dr. Short's office.

Dr. Short called Mrs. Smiley into his office. "Mrs. Smiley, I am putting this case on the back burner until next week. I want to get the views of the board and parents. Is the retreat all set up?" Mrs. Smiley nodded.

The following Saturday found Howard Short sitting in his favorite easy chair on the porch of his camp, a five-thousand-square-foot wooden structure on stilts. The gray-green waters of the Ticktack River flowed silently in front of the screened-in veranda. The long table inside was stacked high with deer meat sausage, cracklings, alligator and turtle dip, sandwiches piled high on a platter, plates of vegetables, crackers, and cheese. A cooler held a variety of diet drinks.

The school board members, a group of teachers, and several parents and community leaders filed in. Each of the individuals invited had come, and they began filling their plates and taking places around the room. Plush couches and deep chairs filled quickly.

Mrs. Kate Fancy, the high school biology teacher, spoke first. "Dr. Short, I read your message and received the package of materials concerning Mr. Wolf. I was shocked to learn that Stephen did not have the doctorate. We all have been calling him 'doctor' since he came to Clinton High two years ago. I guess that's okay: it doesn't really change things. I don't mind his being formal."

"Whether he was formal or not, I have trouble with his 'flying under false colors.' Several other—minority—candidates were passed over, because they were thought to be not as qualified. We need to be fair," Bob Harpole of the NAACP added.

"I agree," Mrs. Filigree Macaster added. "Mr. Wolf—and it is Mr. Wolf and not Dr. Wolf—was hired because it was believed he had the doctorate. We could have hired one of the other candidates two years ago. One was Latino and another African American. They were both good. But we chose Stephen Wolf because he was a doctor. We thought this added something to his credentials that the others did not have. And we went ahead and paid him ten thousand dollars more than Bill Bellows (who only had a master's) because he supposedly had the doctorate and the district pay scale called for more money."

Tom Wilton, from the Citizens Council for Better Schools, broke in. "Listen, this is a matter of false representation. We ought to operate according to principles here. Let's say that if the facts bear out, we will operate according to the rule that falsification of professional work will result in termination!"

"I'm afraid I cannot agree," Dick Frank, a math teacher blurted out. "Wolf has done a fine job as principal. Why, we were headed to the bottom of the district under Bill Bellows. Our test scores were terrible! Stephen Wolf created curriculum teams, formed after-school and week-end tutoring sections for weak students . . . he had us all working to raise scores. You can't beat the success he has generated!"

"Yes, and we are comfortable with Stephen Wolf!" Mrs. Tiffany Hasit, president of the Parent Faculty Association, said. "We parents are happy with how Mr. Wolf is running the ship. Our graduates are going on to fine universities. While only half of the kids thought about college in the past, this last year seventy-five percent of the senior class applied to colleges, and sixty percent got in! I vote to keep Mr. Wolf. If it ain't broke, don't fix it."

Mr. Chancy Albright, one of the social studies teachers, followed up. "He insisted on me referring to him as 'Doctor Wolf.' I was corrected when I referred to him as 'Mr.' during the first faculty meeting! I recall our previous principal, Bill Bellows, wanted us to call him 'Bill.' . . . Quite a difference. Wolf wanted formalities. That's okay, though. You got to do whatever it takes to get things done. Call yourself 'king' if you want. Just get the job done!"

"Hell's Bells!" Martin Buckle, owner of Buckle's Car Emporium, spat out. "I've been a board member for eighteen years. Never have I seen the likes of this. If Wolf gets away with lying on his professional record, we will have everyone doing it. How can you expect our students and teachers to tell the truth on their resumes or anywhere else, if the leader of the school is dishonest about his accomplishments? Why, if any of my employees lied about how many cars they sold, or how much they brought in to the Emporium, I'd fire 'em in a New York minute!"

"Well, I'll just tell you, Howard. Your job's on the line as much as Wolf's is," Sid Poole, school board member and chairman of the Principal Search Committee, stated. "I heard Cecil Weber of KTV telling his camera crew outside as I walked in earlier just that. We have got to think of public opinion here, Howard. Choosing the principals has always been the superintendent's job. We board members have stayed out of it. But, if you do not do what is right, the board will have to act . . . and you may be sending out your own resume!"

"I don't think it amounts to a hill of beans whether he has it or not," Stephanie Fletcher, board member and CEO of EduTV, a public television station, remarked. "Do you need a Ph.D. to run a school? No. If Wolf does his job effectively, and it seems he has, then what are we arguing about? The job description in the advertisement we sent out did not mention a doctorate as either necessary or desirable to be principal. This argument is moot."

"I'm afraid," said Lou Mapleleaf, chairman of the Build It and They Will Come Baseball Stadium Committee, "that if we fire Steve Wolf we will never hear the end of it from our student athletes. Why, he has been behind the new baseball stadium fund-raising efforts big time. Bill Bellows didn't even want baseball...said it took the boys out of too many of their classes! Hog wipes! Why, Steve Wolf was a champion baseball player himself in high school!"

"I'm afraid that is not true," Mrs. Virginia Smiley interjected. "I checked on that, and it seems he never played baseball in high school!" She continued wiping up the dip that had dripped onto the table.

Dale Evers, the Football Dad's president, spoke slowly. "If that's true, maybe we need to look at this more carefully. Can we have two standards here? One standard for the principal, and another for the teachers and kids? What kind of educator offers this as a model to learn from? There is no one more important to a school than the principal. If he or she cheats, lies, or treats others unfairly—well, do we need that kind of character lesson for our kids? He sets a bad example. Our football players need to learn sportsmanship, fair play . . . They don't get those lessons from a fraud and a liar. No, he has got to go!"

The alligator dip was gone; all the cans of diet soda were empty soldiers on the tables and next to the chairs. A few crackers were left on one platter near an exhausted cheese knife. Superintendent Short thanked everyone for attending the retreat and the guests bade each other goodbye. The motors from the speedboats made it difficult to talk. But as the guests shook his hand, Dr. Short had the feeling they had input into the controversy. Mrs. Smiley was the last to leave. She had a warm smile on her face. "See you Monday," she said as she walked down the steps to her car.

—

Analysis

Here we shall review the steps of analysis set forth in chapter 8 and apply them to this case.

Step 1. Gain Knowledge and Understanding

Dr. Short needs to get the facts! Finding out as much as possible about the particular case you must deal with is vital. Interview the participants and eyewitnesses, review printed materials and view documents, phone or speak with reliable sources, and get a clear picture of what the limits of your authority may be in this kind of case.

Do not overdo this part of your job. Some leaders think that if they can just find one more fact or the final shred of evidence, the entire decision will be made for them. This is false comfort. You must gather as many of the pertinent facts as you can and then be satisfied that you can make a decision. It may be that some golden piece of evidence might have swayed the decision the other way, but let that be a matter for the appeals processes.

A. Interview Affected Parties

Two groups emerged in the course of the investigation: The pro Wolf group and the anti-Wolf group. The majority of the school board members at the retreat, and a few parents, felt that Mr. Wolf misrepresented himself on his resume and should not be allowed to continue in his present job. One parent, Dale Evers, believed that Wolf was a poor role model for the students. Members of the group who had been involved in hiring Wolf believed he was a liar. Some people felt that Mr. Wolf lied to them and could not be trusted.

A second group did not think that Mr. Wolf's lying on his resume was that important a matter. A few parents and teachers argued that it did not really make a difference because Mr. Wolf was doing an effective job. Test scores were up. More students were going on to college. A new baseball stadium was in the works. For these people the good that Wolf had done far outweighed the indiscretion he committed when he falsified his credentials.

Table 1 Anti-Mr. Wolf

Name/Position	Argument
Dr. Roland Smart Dean of State Graduate School	. . . fire him . . . would do that in the university.
Mr. Bob Harpole NAACP Leader	. . . several other minority candidates were passed over because they were thought to be not as qualified. That's wrong! We need to do things fairly [Justice]
Mrs. Filagree Macaster Parent	Mr. Wolf was hired because it was believed he had the doctorate. We could have hired one of the other candidates . . .
Tom Wilton Citizens Council for Better Schools	. . . false representation . . . we need to operate according to a rule that falsification of professional work will result in termination. [Deontologist]
Martin Buckle School Board Member	. . . we will have everyone doing it [lying on resume] . . . can't expect teachers and students to be honest if the principal is a liar. . . [Teleologist]
Sid Poole School Board Member & Chairman of the Principal Search Committee	[get rid of Wolf, or you will be fired]
Mr. Dale Evers Football Dad's Club President	two standards: one for the principal (lies) and one for teachers and students? No, athletes need a role model. Fire him.

At stake in the argument over what to do about Mr. Wolf were two contending factions: One group willing to excuse Wolf, and a second group wishing to relieve him of his duties. Short noted that someone brought up the point that the job description for District 812 principal did not call for a Ph.D., in which case she believed the entire matter was moot.

Table 2 For Mr. Wolf

Name/Position	Argument
Stephen Wolf Principal	. . . never bothered to correct people when they called me 'doc.' . . . needed a break from classes . . . I was working on my degree. It's just a misunderstanding. I am doing a great job. I need this job.
Mrs. Kate Fancy Biology Teacher	I was shocked. We just fell in line and called him "doctor." I guess that's alright.
Dick Frank Math Teacher	Wolf created curriculum teams, formed after-school and week-end tutoring . . . had us all working to raise test scores . . .
Mrs. Tiffany Hasit President PFA	We parents are happy with how Mr. Wolf is running the ship . . . our graduates are going on to fine universities... If it ain't broke, don't fix it.
Mr. Chancy Albright Social Studies Teacher	[Wolf] was insecure! I say whatever it takes to get things done. Calling yourself 'king' is fine, if you think it helps get the job done.
Ms Stephanie Fletcher Board Member CEO of public TV station	. . . you don't need a Ph.D. to run a school . . . we never mentioned the doctorate in the job description for principal . . . argument is moot.
Lou Mapleleaf Chairman of Baseball Stadium Committee	. . . if you fire Wolf, student athletes will rebel. Wolf is champion high school baseball player himself [false]

B. Read Related Documents

Howard Short believed that there was a battle going on over conflicting dispositions or attitudes among the people affected by Wolf's resume. He recalled the standards that had been published by ISLLC. He remembered Standard 5, the ethics standard. It called for a teacher or administrator to "play by the rules." Mr. Wolf had not played by the rules of professionals in education: he had lied on his resume. This was unethical from a professional perspective.

C. Collect Material Evidence

Dr. Short carefully took the copy of Mr. Wolf's resume from the materials on his desk and placed it in the special folder he created to contain information and material from the case. The resume was date-stamped. The letter from the dean of the Graduate School stating Wolf had never received the Ph.D. degree was placed in the folder. A letter from Mr. Wolf to the school board members and Search committee chairman Sid Poole was inserted in the folder as well. Finally, Dr. Short took all the votes cast and the letters of recommendation surrounding Wolf's appointment and filed them away. He concluded that the paper trail was adequate to the task of showing that Mr. Wolf's resume was fictitious when it came to his having the Ph.D. when he applied for the job. Dr. Short placed the folder in the vault and locked the door.

D. Determine Relevant Policies

In this case, an educator employed by a school district is thought to have misrepresented his work and experience on his resume. No state or school district policy or rule covers this indiscretion. Dr. Short does discover a professional group's code of conduct for educational administrators on a website. It specifically indicts practicing administrators for lying.

Step 2 Identify Elements of the Issue

A. Determine Problem Area and Issue

Dr. Short would be correct in placing this case within the problem area of education and professionalism, since it seems to involve a misrepresentation of this employee's professional work. The issue is academic honesty (or dishonesty), because the debates Howard Short witnessed accepted the falsification of his resume, yet questioned its importance in terms of his effectiveness.

Lying about your work is an unprofessional thing to do. Codes of professional conduct uniformly label dishonesty as unethical. We would find related moral and ethical infractions in the domain of avoidance of professional duty or misappropriating the office of principal, superintendent, teacher, and so on. A dilemma or issue emerges: Is Mr. Wolf unprofessional if he lied about his professional preparation in securing the job of principal?

B. Find Conflicting Points of View

In this part of Step 2, the leader identifies the various points of contention (competing sides of a fundamental disagreement on two or more courses of action).

Two views seem to be expressed here. One group argues that Mr. Wolf is guilty of falsifying his resume, not something an educator should do. The other group believes that Mr. Wolf may have made a mistake by misrepresenting himself on his resume, but it does not warrant his termination. Of course, there are always some people who sit on the fence or simply say, "I don't know."

Step 3. Reflect
A. *Determine Personal Moral and Ethical Position and Leadership Style*
Dr. Short's personal moral and ethical philosophy was naturalism. He considered all sides of this case and used both the creative and scientific methods. Also, he exemplified by his actions that he believed a practical ethics was the best kind of ethical leadership for today's schools and society.

His leadership style placed him within the school we would call reflective leadership. Dr. Short continued to operate like a scientific and creative problem solver.

B. *Select Appropriate Dispositions or Attitudes*
Dr. Short was disposed to be fair and impartial in the present case. He believed Rawls's theory to best explain the present circumstances and what he ought to do. Short was concerned that he be just, exercise temperance in his judgment, and be honest and forthright in his announcement after the decision.

C. *Lay Out Options*
Dr. Short thought about the choices he had available: Either to forgive the falsified resume and keep Mr. Wolf on, or to terminate him on the grounds that he broke his professional word.

D. *Trace Likely Consequences of Each Option*
If Dr. Short retained Mr. Wolf, he would set a precedent for others who might wish to lie on their official documents. Teachers and students might begin reporting their work in inflated and incorrect terms. The school's reputation as a moral and ethical institution would be harmed. Quality would suffer.

On the other hand, if he terminated him, Mr. Wolf would probably get another job. He would not be "blackballed" for misrepresenting himself. He had good experience and had done a fine job in other administrative positions.

Howard had always respected the notion of doing the least harm as a leader, but here he had to make a decision and the results were embarrassing and difficult any way he looked at it.

Step 4. Make Decision

Dr. Short decided to recommend to the school board that Mr. Wolf be terminated because he had violated the code of professional conduct by misrepresenting his education and preparation for the job of principal. Also, this kind of dishonesty is academic in nature, serving to influence fellow principals, teachers, and students. Were he allowed to lie on his resume, students could not be criticized for lying on their college or job applications, teachers could falsify information on their work experience, and other principals could not be held to honest reporting of their work experience. The trickle-down effects were so overriding that Superintendent Short could not allow this case to pass without punishing Mr. Wolf in some way. The most logical way was to remove him from his post.

To those parents, fellow teachers, and community supporters who thought Wolf was a good principal even though he lied on his resume, Howard Short had the duty to educate. He had to demonstrate to them through communications of various sorts that the good of the school would have been compromised by allowing Mr. Wolf to continue in his job without punishment. For each critic he needed to be prepared to demonstrate the harm Mr. Wolf's actions had and would have if left unaddressed.

Step 5. Live with Decision and Learn from It

No leadership decision is ever made without criticisms. Howard Short needs to understand that moral and ethical decisions are not special in this regard. They must be made in practical and natural ways, but these ways can be improved by study and practice. As Howard Short develops as a school leader, the knowledge, understanding, dispositions, and strategies he brings into play to solve moral and ethical quandaries form his own moral character and the moral character of the school. He is a model of morality and ethics for his principals, teachers, students, and staff. Successful leading with an eye to morals and ethics is different from mere management or administration. Moral and ethical leaders are groundbreakers and true leaders as the choices they make lend strength and character to themselves and to their schools.

Appendix B

The Case of the Undeserved Scholarship

Math teacher Dennis Boudreaux ran his fingers along the edge of the file folder. Juanita's request bothered him. She was a student in his College Algebra II course and was not doing well. He opened the manila folder and pulled out a copy of her program with grades. She had dropped out of Centerdale High in her sophomore year to have a baby. She had been readmitted the following year. Her course grades were average—a C+ overall before dropping out, and a C– since readmission. Attendance records indicated that she had missed quite a number of days of school, but not enough to be flagged as truant. Mrs. Kinwehelp, the guidance counselor, had a number of reports in the file that discussed Juanita's difficulties (single mother, minority family situation, welfare, etc.).

The note from Juanita Perez asked Dennis Boudreaux to write a letter of recommendation for her to receive the MainStep Scholarship. The MainStep Scholarship had been created by Pluntifica and Roger Main, the wife and son of Alvin Main, in his memory. The elder Main had been a student at Centerdale High, then a pre-med student at State University, located in their hometown, when he was drafted during the Korean War. He was killed in battle. Roger Main's great-grandmother had been an Arapaho Indian. The scholarship was need based and designed to help one minority student from Centerdale High who wishes to attend State University, located five miles from Centerdale High. The student must major in a health-related field. The scholarship to State University covers his or her college tuition and books, plus $2,000 per year for four years.

As Dennis flipped through the documents, Juanita seemed to be a student who was disadvantaged. The social worker had a long file on Juanita: Her

173

mother, with whom she lived, was from Puerto Rico and spoke very little English. Juanita's father had left the family when Juanita was six years of age. Juanita had a younger brother, Louis (sixteen), and two sisters (one fifteen and the other fourteen). Mrs. Perez mopped floors in the BANK-TOO building downtown. Louis Perez was the star quarterback for Centerdale High. Recently, recruiters from State University had been observed visiting football practice sessions. Louis worked at The Big Burger on the weekends, and Juanita and her sisters baby-sat in their spare time for money.

The folder contained more notes. Juanita's brother, Louis, had been involved in a fight after school at the local Dairy King when he was fourteen. The police had to be called. Juanita's score on the Sophomore Jump Test, which she took before she dropped out of school, placed her in the bottom half of her class. An I.Q. test revealed a score of 113. Dennis read her MainStep essay. She mentioned how difficult it was to feed all the children in the family and how they had to go to the Food Bank to get groceries. The landlord had twice threatened to put them out on the street if they did not pay the rent. Juanita's career goal was to become a nurse. Her mother's and brother's salaries amounted to $13,500 a year. The poverty jumped out at Dennis as he read the essay. Clearly, there was a need here.

Dennis believed Juanita could be admitted to State U. but might have difficulty completing an undergraduate degree. After all, State University had just raised admission standards and now was blocking returning students from being admitted to some colleges based upon their recent grade point averages. Supported or not, Dennis saw a track record of average performance on standardized tests and in regular classes. Her family responsibilities might have slowed her down.

Dennis picked up a second file folder with the name 'Trinca Jones' printed on the flap. Trinca had been in Dennis's homeroom, had taken his Trig course the semester before, and was senior class president. The Jones family was prominent in the community. Mr. Carl Jones had owned the State Line Lumber Company, building it up from a few sticks to the largest lumber company in the state! A few years ago, with much notoriety, Carl Jones had created a trust and retired from the company he had created. He was now the chairman of the board of State Line at a yearly salary of $1.00. Dennis knew that wealthy people often use a "trust" to avoid income taxes. Trinca's statement of family finances revealed that the Jones's taxable income was less than $15,000 for the previous year.

Mrs. Patricia Jones, Trinca's mother, was the president of the Centerdale

Temps, a business that provides temporary office workers to local businesses. This company was owned by the State Line Trust. Patricia also headed up the Centerdale Quilt & Care Society, which had sent over 1,000 quilts to victims of earthquakes and floods in the last two years. She was subdeacon in the Reformed Naturalist Church, where she sang in the choir. Trinca's older brother, Tred, was in medical school in Spain. Dennis had heard that Tred's tuition alone was $25,000 per year. He had received no scholarships (somehow State Line Trust had picked up his costs). Tred had chosen the school because it was the best in Down syndrome, a malady that had caused his younger brother to be institutionalized. Trinca was quite close to Charlie, her younger brother with Down syndrome, and worked with him each day after school. Therapists at Centerdale Home for Exceptional Children credited Trinca with helping her brother to learn the skills he would need as an adult. The Jones's plan was to place Charlie in a halfway house the following year. Clearly, Trinca would wish to stay in the region to aid Charlie in this move. A younger sister, Felice, was in the Centerdale Elementary School where she had been an outstanding student.

The guidance counselor, Mrs. Kinwehelp, had notes in Trinca's folder as well. One note was a report on her I.Q., which unofficially placed her in the genius category. Another memo commented on Trinca's student deportment during the previous year: every teacher interviewed ranked her as having "Highest" in the moral and ethical traits area. Her scores on the Sophomore Jump Test were in the top 5 percent.

Certainly, Trinca could succeed in college (with her record and I.Q.), Dennis thought. Yet, he was concerned. Trinca was from an "advantaged home," even if her parents' tax statement did not reveal this fact. Despite documents, Trinca seemed to stretch the meaning of the "need" criterion of the scholarship.

Dennis read her essay. She mentioned two trips to Europe and an experience the previous summer helping to build a home for people in a poor Indian village in northern Canada. She expressed a desire to become a physician so that she might return to serve the Indians in Canada. Given Trinca's intelligence and drive, there was no doubt she would successfully complete her bachelor's degree from State University and go on to medical school, Dennis thought.

He closed the folders and placed them side by side. The rules of the MainStep Committee were that he would be allowed to write only one letter in support of a student. He cracked his knuckles as he pondered his choice of what to do.

Notes

Dennis Boudreaux's name has been mentioned by the superintendent during the last board meeting. He might be selected to be a part of the first "Leadership Cohort" to work on their master's degree in educational leadership at State University. If he were chosen, the district would cover all of his expenses. Dennis felt his behavior was under scrutiny by the upper administration. He had always been a loyal employee and mindful of his duties.

The superintendent, an avid football fan, was one of three members of the MainStep Scholarship Committee along with Roger and Pluntifica Main. Dennis knew that anything he might write would be examined carefully with an eye to his future role as a principal in the district.

Pluntifica Main bowled each Thursday evening with Trinca Jones's mother, Mrs. Patricia Jones. Patricia's husband, Carl, worked late each Thursday in the BANK-TOO Building, where Mrs. Perez, Juanita's mother, mopped his floor. He had been in the habit of bringing Mrs. Perez some of his children's cast-off clothing every so often. She was a fabulous cook and often shared some of her dinners with Carl Main in appreciation. He particularly loved her taco grande!

Dennis spoke fluent Cajun French. His grandfather had a third-grade education. Blanco Boudreaux had been expelled from Bayou River Elementary School in the 1930s for speaking French, and he never returned.

Questions for Further Consideration

Work through the five steps of analysis: (1) Gather knowledge and understanding of the case; (2) Identify the problem area, issue, and conflicting points of view; (3) Reflect about your personal moral and ethical position, options, and likely consequences of your choice; (4) Make a decision; (5) How would you live with and learn from your decision? Make particular reference to the following concerns:

1. Of course, Dennis does not have to write a letter for either one of these students. Or does he? Is it a responsibility of teachers to write letters of recommendation if asked to do so by former students? What reasons may be offered for not writing a letter in this case?

2. Recall what John Rawls has written about equality and fairness. How does this attitude come into play here? What rules or principles can be appealed to in dealing with this decision?

3. What does the caring attitude mean for this case? What data support the possibility of caring being employed in this case? What would the model of "least harm" mean for this decision?

4. How may Dennis be concerned with the consequences of his choice for the two young students? Are the students' rights involved? What will be the effects on the common good of the school if he decides for Juanita over Trinca, or vice versa?

5. Dennis sees himself as a future leader (principal) in his school district. How may his decision affect his future as a principal? What image of leadership may inform his decision in this case? How might his moral character be affected by his choice?

6. What would you decide in this case and why would you decide in this way?

Appendix C

The Case of Unintended Harm

Stanleyville was a quiet community in the northern part of the state. Most of the adults were employed in the local factories and businesses. You might say that Stanleyville was middle class. The Constance Elementary School was one of five schools peppered throughout the town. The children were middle class.

Mr. Carl Clutter was a new assistant principal at Constance Elementary School and had recently received his master's degree in educational administration from State University. An elementary-level math teacher and coach of the track team, Carl found little spare time for his wife of five years and their one-year-old child. Nevertheless, he was often at school in the evenings and on weekends. Mrs. Elvira Madigan, the principal for the past ten years, had been at Constance for twenty-five years. She rose from being a home economics teacher to principal. Most people would agree that she was something of an "absentee landlord," for she was rarely visible outside of her office. She liked a "tight ship," and recruited Mr. Clutter because of his size and deep voice. He was just the kind of authority figure she needed for her assistant principal.

When Elsie Divine, the fourth grade teacher, came into his office early on a Friday morning, Carl did not know what to make of it. He had been on the job only a few short weeks, and besides the formal introduction given him by Mrs. Madigan, he really had not met with the teachers about any of the issues he wished to address as their new AP. Elsie had known Carl because she had gone to school with Carl's wife, Lori, and they attended the First Refined Church together. She seemed upset.

"Carl, I have a little problem!"

"Yes, Elsie. What is it?" Carl asked.

"Well, one of my students. She, that is, Marjorie Marks, came to school today with a gun. Well, not really a gun, but it is a violation!"

"Please explain, Elsie. What gun?"

"Marjorie comes to school herself each day. She often stops at the Pick-a-Pac on her way. I've seen her in there. Anyway, today, as she explained it to me, she put a quarter into one of those gum ball machines and out came a toy gun. It isn't very big, but it is a gun. And, you know we have zero tolerance for such things on campus!"

"I understand the principal's feelings about the zero tolerance rule. Superintendent Smith got the board to pass that policy last summer. We have a compliance document in our records."

Elsie was visibly upset as she continued. "I don't want to turn her in, but the students saw the gun. They told me she had it. It is a little miniature cap gun without the caps. A toy gun. But . . . well, you know . . . I had to tell someone in authority. You know, Marjorie is a great little girl. She has not had it easy at home lately. And she isn't fitting in with the rest of the girls in the class. Marjorie doesn't have the nice clothes some of them have. I really feel sorry for her. . . . Here it is."

Elsie thrust her clenched fist at Carl and unwrapped her fingers, slowly revealing a shiny rough-looking toy gun about two inches long. Carl gazed down at the little metal object, flipping the trigger back and forth. It looked like one of the old guns women in the Wild West carried in their purses. It was convincing.

"Thank you for bringing this in, Elsie. I appreciate your confiding in me. Can you have Marjorie come to my office? You probably need to get back to your class."

Elsie nodded, rose, and turned. As she walked toward the door, she looked back with tears in her eyes.

A few minutes later, nine-year-old Marjorie knocked on the door and Carl motioned her to come in and sit down.

"Please sit down, Marjorie. Mrs. Divine gave me something she said you brought to school today. . . ."

Marjorie began to cry. "Honest, Mr. Clutter, I didn't know I was being bad. I won that toy gun. I never win nothin' and this time I won! I wasn't goin' to leave it there. I mean, I won it, I made those claws just drop right down on that toy gun and pick it up! I wanted to keep it. Mr. Styles, the Pick-a-Pac man, said I should take it to school and show my friends. . . . He said he never had seen anybody win anything out of that machine! That silly Sally Neverfield told on me! I wasn't goin' to hurt anybody!"

"I see. Well, Marjorie, we have a rule against bringing weapons on the school grounds, any kind of weapon, even a toy. You knew that, didn't you?"

"Yes, but this was different. I had it in my sack. I wasn't goin' to show it to no one. Sally was peeking. She told Mrs. Divine."

"Okay. But I am going to have to phone your parents. They will have to come down to school about this."

"Please, please, Mr. Clutter, don't call my dad. He'll be upset with me. . . ." Little Marjorie began to weep uncontrollably.

Carl took the child's hand and led her out of the room and back down to her classroom.

When he returned to his office he phoned the social worker, who came right over. She pulled at her large leather folder and her files and said that Marjorie had come to school bruised several times. The parents had been investigated for child abuse. The father was unemployed and had a drinking problem. The mother was a dropout from high school and had worked as an exotic dancer until she met the father. Now with her husband out of work, she had returned to the strip and was employed in her previous job. With no one at home, the social worker said she had been concerned for Marjorie.

Carl looked at the file she passed to him. Marjorie had excellent grades in the first three years, but her grades were low this past semester. Written comments by her teacher indicated that Marjorie was having trouble concentrating, daydreamed in class, and failed to get her assignments in on time. She was not a discipline problem. Marjorie's one close friend had moved to another state with her parents. The social worker's comments were recorded in a neat print; the episodes of bruises were recorded and the nurse's remarks were all there.

Carl thanked the social worker as she left the office.

He sat and thought deeply about the case and formed his decision.

Questions for Further Consideration

Work through the five steps of analysis: (1) Gather knowledge and understanding of the case; (2) Identify the problem area, issue, and conflicting points of view; (3) Reflect about your personal moral and ethical position, leadership style, options, and likely consequences of your choice; (4) Make a decision; (5) How would you live with and learn from your decision? Make particular reference to the following concerns:

1. Could Carl Clutter have handled this incident any differently?

2. Should Carl speak to the principal, Mrs. Madigan, about this case? If so, how should he frame his remarks?

3. The facts were clear. Marjorie Marks had brought a weapon (even though a toy) onto the school grounds and that was a violation of the policy of zero tolerance. But what if she had been told by an adult to do so? Is she responsible for her actions then?

4. We wish to locate blame, but if no one is hurt, is there any blame to be assigned?

5. If Carl Clutter calls her parents, Marjorie may suffer the consequences of her father's anger. Is this a reason for not phoning the parents and dealing with this case at the school?

6. If Carl does not call her parents, Marjorie may actually not be treated fairly or in a just manner. If justice is even, then anyone who violates the policy deserves to be punished.

7. Justice needs to be tempered by mercy, Carl thought. He paraphrased a line from Shakespeare's play, The Merchant of Venice: "The quality of mercy should not be strained . . ." Caring was important, he thought.

8. What should Carl Clutter do? What is his decision to be? And on what ethical theory is it to be based?

Appendix D

The Case of the Gun in the High School

During the early weeks of the fall semester, sixteen-year-old Clyde Day boarded the bus to travel to school when it stopped at the end of his road. He was tense and his eyes were focused straight ahead as he walked up the aisle and took a seat midway in the bus. Clyde sat with his feet outstretched into the aisle. Two of his friends tried to engage him in conversation, but Clyde sat motionless as if in a trance. John Fine, one of the boys he liked to play basketball with, probed Clyde. "What's the matter, Clyde?"

The sullen boy replied, "Nothin." The bus rounded the last curve and pulled into its regular unloading station. Clyde got up. He clutched his waist as he walked down the steps of the bus and toward the West Elevation High School. John ran up beside him.

"You've got something goin' on, Clyde . . . why don't you unload."

"Hell, John. That damn Mr. Sparks gave me another detention, and Billy Fudd got the class a-laughin' at me! I'm goin' to blow their XX@## heads off!"

Clyde pulled back his shirt to reveal a cold steel revolver stuck in his pants. The black handle grips were worn gray but shone in the light of the morning.

"Hell, you say!" said John. "Don't ya know ya can get into big trouble bringing a gun to school?"

The bigger youth stopped and pulled up his trouser leg to reveal a silver clip sticking out of his shoe. "I got the ammunition . . . and I aim to kick their #@$$!"

John knew that Clyde liked Sindee Lou. He motioned to her to come over. She looked at the pair, sensed trouble, and asked, "What's the matter?" Clyde looked down at the ground.

John pointed to Clyde. "Clyde . . . he be sayin' he wants to blast Billy Fudd and Mr. Sparks!"

"What? You nuts!" She dropped her backpack on the concrete in front of the entrance to the school. "They'll take you to jail!"

Clyde pulled his arm free of John Fine's grip. "Let me go . . . I got work to do." He strode through the doors and into the main hallway of the school. He walked briskly out of sight. John and Sindee Lou looked after him in amazement.

"Clyde's lost it. . . . We got to do somethin'," Sindee Lou said. As they hurried down the hall to Mr. Sparks's room, Sarah Jewel ran up to them. "That goofy Clyde's got a gun! I saw him stuff it under the Coke machine!" Sarah pulled at Sindee Lou's arm. "Come on, girl! We've got to tell someone!"

John and Sindee stopped. John blurted out, "No, wait. If we tell on him, he'll go to jail. Maybe he's just bluffin'."

"Bluffin' hell . . . I seen him take the eyes out of a squirrel at two hundred yards. Clyde's mean with a gun. And he is mad as hell!"

The three students stood transfixed. Finally, Sindee broke the silence. "Look, that gun is okay while it's under the machine. We got to tell Mr. Sparks or somebody. . . . If he takes it out and loads it, he will do something crazy. You know Clyde. He's a hothead if ever there was one."

The three walked toward Mr. Sparks, who stood outside his classroom. "Mornin', kids." Mr. Sparks always seemed so happy. He had three small kids. His wife had been killed by a train when she stalled on the B. & O. tracks up near the sawmill a year ago September. The loss was written on his face. Yet he had decided to try to make his way by doing extra teaching in the summer and helping out at the day care on Sunday mornings. His church had helped him a lot in getting through the ordeal.

Sindee thought of Mr. Sparks's three small children and how they would miss their daddy if Clyde killed him. She pictured Clyde walking into the classroom, pulling back his big coat and shooting Mr. Sparks, blood flying everywhere, students screaming and diving for the floor. The scene faded into a movie she had seen in which another student did the same thing. He wore a big Australian long coat and he had a big rifle. Clyde's face was super-imposed on the actor's. Suddenly the movie and West Elevation High came together. She stopped herself.

John thought of the day he and Clyde beat South High's famous five on the basketball court last February. They couldn't miss a shot. John tossed the ball up on the backboard and big Clyde leaped up and dunked it! What a pair they were. The sportswriter from the city had written them up as the "Click and Clack of B Ball." They played in the "B" league that season. Now they were both looking at being on the senior team. He pushed events into the future. If Clyde killed somebody, Clyde would not be able to play ball. He, John, would not have a partner. The team would suffer, the school would suffer, and John saw his scholarship to State going up in flames. Sindee nudged him back to reality.

Sarah Jewel knew she was no rocket scientist. After barely getting through her sophomore year, she was facing the junior year with fear. But this Clyde business was bad. She recalled the summer she had spent at Camp Daffy Dale when she was about thirteen. That had been so much fun. The camp counselor was an older gal from State. They had had lots of campfire chats that summer. She recalled the time Betty told the campers a story and then asked each one to finish it out loud.

The story went something like this: "A very poor man had a very sick wife. She needed some expensive medicine. The man went to the drugstore and asked the druggist for the medicine, but he did not have enough money to pay for it. Frustrated, he went home and thought. He decided to . . . " Most of the girls said that he should steal it. A few said that he should go and get a job and earn the money and then buy the medicine.

The next night, she told another story: "A young man is drafted into the army. His mother is very ill and she relies upon him and his salary to live. The army calls him to service. When several military policemen appear at the front door one night, he . . ." This time most of the girls said he should hide. But Sarah said that since serving his country was the law of the land, he should have gone with them. She was somehow proud of her decision.

Sarah Jewel thought about Clyde and the situation she faced: If she did not tell on Clyde, he might kill someone. Killing people was wrong. Clyde would be violating a commandment from the Bible. She liked Clyde, but he had to be stopped before he broke this biblical law.

Questions for Further Consideration

Work through the five steps of analysis (1) Gather knowledge and understanding of the case; (2) Identify the problem area, issue, and conflicting points of view; (3) Reflect about your personal moral and ethical position, options, and likely consequences of your choice; (4) Make a decision; (5) How would you live with and learn from your decision? Make particular reference to the following concerns:

1. Consider this case from a national and regional perspective. What recent and historical events color the present case? What is the "temper of the times"?

2. Each of the individuals involved (John, Sindee, and Sarah Jewel) provides a rationale for what he or she believe about making a class of decisions. Tell what each person argues and what theory of ethics may support his or her belief.

3. Given the scenario and the possible choices, what would you do if you were: (a) Clyde's mother; (b) Clyde's favorite teacher; (c) Clyde's principal or assistant principal; (d) a local law enforcement officer assigned to the school; or, (e) the district attorney.

4. While serious ethical matters are involved in this case, legal and policy matters need to be addressed as well. Tell what the legal factors may be. How would you as a school principal sort out the moral and ethical issues (care versus justice) from what the law requires in this case?

5. Given the new standards for school leaders, which standard may bear upon this case and compel the principal to act in certain ways? How might you enhance or improve upon the standards that match the case?

Appendix E

The Case of the Dirty Birds

Round Rock High principal Marsha Mason reread the newspaper article from the November 8, 2001, issue of the Baton Rouge *Advocate*.

BOARD BANS "LEWD" CHEERS, DANCES.

SAVANNAH, GA—School officials on Wednesday banned "lewd gestures" and "vulgar movements" from school performances in response to complaints that some cheerleading and dance routines had become too sexy.

The Chatham County School Board voted unanimously, saying the policy strikes a balance by answering offended parents without setting strict standards that put the board in the role of morality police.

"It wasn't like it was widespread," board member Jessie DeLoach Collier said of the complaints. "It's just some people, because of their religion, may have been embarrassed by some of the things they saw."

The policy bans "lewd gestures, inappropriate comments, foul language and suggestive or vulgar movements" at school functions by all student groups, from glee clubs to wrestling teams. Board president Diane Cantor said the final decision of what's tasteful is up to school principals.

She thought, "This is what is happening to me!" A nearly identical situation had developed in her own school district.

It had all started when Mrs. Rita O'Leary announced her retirement last spring. Mrs. O'Leary had been a P.E. teacher and advisor in charge of the cheerleading and dance squads.

When Principal Mason ran an advertisement in the local paper she received two inquiries, one from an individual who had neither a teaching certificate nor experience. The second candidate, Ms. Lou LeFleur, had her teaching credentials and had taught P.E. briefly (for three years) in nearby Coal City before moving to Las Vegas with her husband, who was stationed there.

During Ms. LeFleur's interview with Principal Mason and Assistant Principal Smith, her resume was examined and she answered all questions well.

However, when asked if she could coach the cheerleaders and dancers, Ms. LeFleur rose from her chair to her full six feet, three inches of height, flew high into the air, and came down in a split!

"So, you've had dance experience, have you, Ms. LeFleur?" Principal Mason asked meekly.

"Yes, I have!" replied Lou LeFleur from the floor. "I worked as a Las Vegas entertainer for five years at the Monumental Casino. You know, the one that spews lava every forty-five minutes! Also, I took dance lessons from three years of age right here in Round Rock at the Pope-Moisture School of Dance. And during my high school and college years I was a cheerleader, played on the volleyball team, and was a gymnast. So, yes, . . . I have experience!"

Marsha pulled out a contract and hired her on the spot!

That summer, Ms. LeFleur came in each morning (without pay). She worked hard at cleaning and painting her office, arranging her P.E. course curricula, checking out the gymnastics and volleyball equipment, and laying out a schedule for the cheerleading and dance teams to practice.

Her divorce from her husband Karl had forced her to come home. She was living with her mother, a retired seamstress. Together they had the members of the cheerleading and dance squads come to school for measurements and later fittings. If anything, Ms. LeFleur was organized and knew how to achieve goals.

Lou LeFleur worked hard practicing with the girls on the cheerleading squad and dance team. The girls loved her! They practiced together each afternoon, Ms. LeFleur and the girls all dressed in tights. They worked on routines in the old girl's gym. Soon more girls came to the gym and asked to try out for the teams. Lou was a very popular teacher.

Lou's mother worked frantically to finish the costumes for the first football game.

The first sign of trouble came during the first week of classes. Mrs. Edna Denial phoned Principal Mason to tell her, "My little Cindy came home yesterday with her finished costume and tried it on for the family. Principal Mason, I don't wish to be a complaining parent, but these costumes the dancers are supposed to wear . . . Well, too much of my Cindy is showing! I am concerned . . . they are so brief."

Marsha assured Mrs. Denial she would look into the matter and not to worry. Everything would be "okay." After she hung up she recalled Mrs. O'Leary's 1950s hairstyles for the girls and bell-bottom slacks she had dressed the dancers in for years. Lou LeFleur had probably tossed them out! Also, she recalled Cindy Denial being sent to her office with low hip-huggers and belly-button ring. She had had to send Cindy home to change clothes. Marsha nonetheless made a mental note to speak with Lou LeFleur.

The matter slipped her mind until the first football game. The Round Rock Fighting Blue Jays played the Swamp City Eagles. The Round Rock teams had usually been 0 - 8 for the season, but something good was happening during the first half. The Blue Jays were up 23 to 0! Coach Harlen Ellison was ecstatic! He danced off the field at half time to the Jay's locker room.

During the half-time show, Lou LeFleur stood on the fifty-yard line, dressed in a long blue cape. She nodded to the band and directed her dancers to begin. The girls strode out onto the field in capes and blue jay hats, flipped off the outer garment, and revealed they were clad in blue feathers and strips of blue cloth. They launched into a near professional quality dance routine in which everything seemed to wiggle. The Round Rock band played its heart out. The parents, especially the fathers, stood and applauded until their hands were pink!

After the dance numbers, Mrs. Denial, Cindy's mother, came over to Marsha and blurted out, "Wasn't my Cindy terrific? She was the fourth bird from the left. That Ms. LeFleur has turned a turnip into a rose! Her grades are all A's and she wants to be a *professional* dancer!"

During the second half, the Round Rock team continued to destroy the Swamp City Eagles. The Eagle quarterback became so distracted by the Blue Jay cheerleader captain, Wanda Love, that he threw two perfect passes to her on the sidelines! The game concluded with a score of 64 to 0. Coach Ellison was carried off the field by his players and parents. The goal posts were torn down and one parent volunteered to gold plate the game ball for the Round Rock trophy cabinet.

Principal Mason settled into her chair on Monday morning with a grin that seemed a permanent fixture! First, Coach Ellison phoned to say he was so pleased with the team and Ms. LeFleur for stirring the crowd in support of his boys. He said he had personally sent two dozen roses to her and her teams. And, he promised the team would kill the Darlington Senators the following week.

This call was followed by one from the president of the Boys Athletic Association, Bill Simpson, a big contributor to the sports program at Round Rock High, congratulating her for turning the teams around and the wonderful cheerleading and dance team support at the game. He was contributing $250,000 to the school and she was to do with it what she pleased, but he hoped Ms. LeFleur would be given all new gym equipment and her gym floor would be refinished!

The next phone call came from Mrs. Alice Proper, president of the Moral Minority. Mrs. Proper complained that parents with children in Round Rock High had been phoning her all weekend long to say that the cheerleaders and dancers were making lewd gestures and vulgar movements. She said they wished the dance and cheerleading costumes to be changed back to the bell-bottoms Mrs. O'Leary had used and the routines made "less sexy."

Another call, this time from Mrs. Patience Holloway, complained that her Douglas was in the band, played the tuba, and had to go to the hospital with a double hernia after the football game. He had played himself out! She expressed a concern that maybe the "suggestive routines" by the girls had "overstimulated" some of the young male band members at the game! "Could you look into toning down the dancers?"

The rival coach of the losing Eagles phoned to say that his quarterback had decided to move to Round Rock with his family. He said the next time he played the Blue Jays, he would hire his own Las Vegas dancer to coach his cheerleaders! And, as far as Marsha was concerned, his uncle, who was president of her school board, would fire her if she didn't clean things up there! He then hung up.

That afternoon, Principal Marsha Mason called Ms. Lou LeFleur into her office for "a chat."

"Lou, you have done a great job! You have transformed the cheerleaders and dancers into pros. They will do great in the state competitions, I am certain! You also are a great teacher. I have no complaints about your first-year performance here at Round Rock High.

However, we have been getting calls from parents and others that the dance and cheerleading routines may be . . . well, may be too suggestive! Some people have complained that their routines and outfits are lewd and vulgar."

Lou LeFleur fired back. "Look, Principal Mason, I have taken a group of girls out of the 1950s into the twenty-first century. They are doing nothing lewd or vulgar! In fact, the girls have been studying videotapes of real blue jays and their ordinary and mating behaviors in Mrs. Brown's science class. I took those tapes and choreographed the dance numbers. What you see is what blue jays actually do!"

"But, Lou," Marsha replied, "don't you think the costumes are a bit skimpy?"

"Not by any standards!" Lou retorted. "The square-inch coverage of feathers actually exceeds that of fabric covering cheerleaders and dancers in every other school! The feathers were donated by my girl friends in Las Vegas, all of whom are over six feet tall . . . there is more than enough featherage to cover these shorter high school girls. Besides, the girls are all wearing blue full-length body suits under those feathers! (This is for warmth and for effect.) Even their blue jay hats cover the face like a mask. So, no one can even tell who is who out there on the field!"

Marsha Mason thanked Lou LeFleur for stopping by and concluded the conversation.

Marsha had not thought the costumes or the routines of the cheerleaders and dancers were "dirty" in any way. But, she was not everyone. Some people were upset. The Moral Minority had a big following. They had made life quite difficult for the previous principal of Round Rock.

On the other hand, maybe the offended parents would grow accustomed to the routines and costumes. Maybe the support for the team would lead to their becoming State champs. Maybe the $250,000 would cushion any criticisms, if spent in the right places. The newspapers were suddenly supporters of her school. The facts swam in her head. She rubbed her forehead until it hurt.

The next meeting of the District School Board found members engaging in heated arguments over the cheerleading and dance squads at Round Rock High. Eventually, prompted by one board member who expressed a "religious group's" complaints regarding the costumes and movements of the Round Rock cheerleaders and dancers, they passed a policy that there would be no lewdness or vulgarity expressed by any member of a student group. What was tasteful was to be left up to the principal, however.

What should Marsha Mason do?

Leading Questions

1. What problem area does this case fit? What is the essential issue?
2. Tell what the sides in this argument assert and what reasons they give for their positions.

3. Certainly, both the principal and Ms. LeFleur abide by certain leadership standards and dispositions, and they perform in certain ways: Characterize these.

4. There are many ethical matters at stake in this case. Values fill the case. What is the ethical controversy here? What theories of ethics are at play? What philosophy of ethics has each of the players assumed?

5. What moral standards, dispositions, and performances are at work in this case?

6. What ought Principal Mason to do? Why? What leadership style and ethical philosophy should she adopt? What decision should she make? What are the likely outcomes of this decision?

Appendix F

The Case of Academic Freedom

Mrs. Overit is an English teacher at Happy High School, Big River, Louisiana where she teaches mostly juniors. She has been employed by the Big River School District for eight years. Recently, Mrs. Overit acquired a personal computer that she brought to school and hooked up to the local area network. She began using the computer by allowing students who had finished their regular work to go onto the Internet to look up sources for their "Third Year Theme."

Some weeks later, Mr. Glen Hopkins, the assistant principal, was passing the classroom and happened to look in the window. He noticed Tod Threshold, the junior football quarterback, at the keyboard of the computer. On the computer screen was a screen saver depicting a mass of slimy green snakes. Tod was looking at a notebook on the computer table. When he began typing on the keyboard, the screen saver disappeared and the familiar Internet browser site flashed on the screen.

Eight years ago Mr. Hopkins had dated Mrs. Overit for about six months, when she first arrived as a new teacher (with the name Ms. Serpa N. Tine) at Happy High School. They were enjoying each other's company and appeared to be "an item" around town. Then, rather mysteriously, Ms. Tine and Mr. Hopkins were no longer seen at the bowling alley on Friday evenings drinking chocolate milkshakes, as had been their habit.

Mr. Richard Right, the principal of Happy High, had been in that job for fourteen years. He had observed his assistant principal and Ms. Tine at the bowling alley. When they no longer appeared on Friday nights, he waited for an opportune moment (cleaning the boys' lockers after the last basketball game of the season) and asked Glen Hopkins about Ms. Tine. He said that they had "religious differences" and left it at that.

After his observation of Tod using Serpa Overit's computer, Hopkins walked directly to Principal Right's office. "Richard," Glen Hopkins blurted out, "Serpa has objectionable material on her computer!" Richard Right sat up straight. His brass duck flew off his desk onto the floor. "What?"

"I was passing her room, looked in, and there was Tod Threshold using her computer. There were all these slimy snakes on the screen!"

"Well, so . . . ?"

"Mrs. Overit is a snake worshipper, that's what! She belongs to one of those cults. She believes that snakes cure illness. I guess she got indoctrinated when she was a kid in Harold's Hollow. You know, you learn from your mother's knee. Serpa had a snake-loving momma!"

"What do you propose?" Richard Right asked.

"It's simple. She needs to be written up. That darn snake stuff needs to be dug out of that computer! She has been using school district money to run that computer. Taxpayers are paying for her to indoctrinate those students with all that snake religion stuff! This is a public school. Teachers can't do that!" Glen Hopkins turned on his heel and stomped out of the office.

Principal Right knew he should call Serpa to the office and discuss this issue, so he had Mrs. Flaming send a student down to Serpa's classroom. In a few moments, Serpa stood in the doorway of Richard Right's outer office. Her eyes passed over his collection of *Field & Stream* and *BassFisher* magazines piled next to the short couch in the waiting room outside his office. On the walls were prints of ducks in flight and hunters with raised guns. A large paperweight covered some reports on the coffee table. The plastic paperweight had a small alligator inside with its mouth open.

Principal Right motioned Serpa into his office. "Sit down, Serpa." Right pointed to the leather chair in front of his desk. Behind Richard Right, on the wall, was an enormous deer's head. On his desk was a plastic fish. Serpa had seen this novelty fish in the Bigmart. If you pressed a button it would flip its tail, turn its head, and say something humorous.

"Serpa, I don't want to upset you," Richard Right began. "But, there have been complaints that you have a rather strange screen saver on your computer in your classroom. Do you want to talk about this?"

Serpa drew herself up and folded her hands smartly on her lap. "No, I don't see what my screen saver has to do with teaching and learning! I'll bet it was that worm Glen Hopkins! He has been looking for anything he can find to nail me and my reputation. Ever since he dropped me!"

Serpa's eyes began to tear. Richard Right felt uncomfortable.

"Well, Serpa, I have a complaint that you are displaying religious material on your computer. It has also been claimed that this material is being presented to the students in your classroom. Now, I don't want to have to write you up on this. . . . "

Serpa locked her jaw and looked deeply into Richard Right's eyes. "Look, Principal Right, I am no more pushing religion than you are with all these darn dead animals and things in your office. Why pick on me? I don't want to be written up. If you write me up, I will take it to the board! I'm an animal rights person, and I find all this celebration of animal misery in your office to be offensive! You're the one who should be written up!"

Serpa jumped up and stormed out of Richard Right's office.

Questions for Further Consideration

Work through the five steps of analysis: (1) Gather knowledge and understanding of the case; (2) Identify the problem area, issue, and conflicting points of view; (3) Reflect about your personal moral and ethical position, leadership style, options, and likely consequences of your choice; (4) Make a decision; (5) How would you live with and learn from your decision? Make particular reference to the following concerns:

1. What has the A.A.U.P. (American Association of University Professors) said about issues of Academic Freedom? Visit their website and review their position papers on this matter.
2. The new technologies now available in schools are having an impact upon academic freedom. How does technology play a special role in this case?
3. What rights are involved in this case?
4. Is there a standard or code item that regulates such matters?

References

Alexander, C., H. Neis, A. Anninou, & I. King (1987). *A new theory of urban design*. New York: Oxford University Press.

Alexander, T. M. (1987). *John Dewey's theory of art, experience and nature: The horizons of feeling*. Albany, NY: SUNY Press.

Aristotle (1980). *Nicomachean ethics* (W. D. Ross, Trans.). New York: Oxford University Press.

Arons, S. (1997). *Short route to chaos*. Amherst, MA: University of Massachusetts Press.

Ausbaugh, C. R. & K. L. Kasten (1991). *Educational leadership: Case studies in reflective practice*. New York: Longman.

Badiou, A. (2001). *Ethics: An essay on the understanding of evil*. (P. Hallward, Trans.) London: Verso.

Barnard, C. I. (1938). *Functions of the executive*. Cambridge, MA: Harvard University Press.

Bateson, M. C. (1989). *Composing a life*. New York: Atlantic Monthly Press.

Baumeister, R. F. (1998). The self. In D. T. Gilbert, S. T. Fiske, & G. Lindzey (Eds.), *The handbook of social psychology* (Vol. 1, 4th ed.). Boston: McGraw-Hill.

Beck, L. G. (1994). *Reclaiming educational administration as a caring profession*. New York: Teachers College Press.

Beck, L. G. & J. Murphy (1994). *Ethics in educational leadership programs: An expanding role*. Thousand Oaks, CA: Corwin-Sage.

Beck, L. G. & J. Murphy, & Associates (1997). *Ethics in educational leadership programs: Emerging models*. Columbia, MO: University Council for Educational Administration.

Benn, P. (1998). *Ethics*. Montreal: McGill University Press.

Bennett, N. & A. Harris (1999). Hearing truth from power? Organisation theory, school effectiveness and school improvement. *School Effectiveness and School Improvement, 10* (4), 533–550.

Bennett, W. J. (ed.) (1989). *The book of virtues: A treasury of great moral stories*. New York: Touchstone.

Beyer, L. E. (1997). The moral contours of teacher education. *Journal of Teacher Education*, 48(4), 243–254.

Beyer, L. E. & D. P. Liston (1992). Discourse or moral action? A critique of postmodernism. *Educational Theory*, 42(4), 371–393.

Bidney, D. (1967). *Theoretical anthropology*. New York: Schocken Books.

Bull, B. L., R. T. Fruehling & V. Chattergy (1992). *The ethics of multicultural and bilingual education*. New York: Teachers College Press.

Butler, J. A. & K. M. Dickson (1987). Improving school culture: Centennial High School. School Improvement Research Series (SIRS), Portland, OR. Northwest Regional Educational Laboratory. http://www.nwrel.org/scpd /sirs/1/snap2.html.

Callahan, R. (1961). *Education and the cult of efficiency*. Chicago: University of Chicago Press.

Campbell, J. (1992). *The community reconstructs: The meaning of pragmatic social thought*. Urbana, IL: University of Illinois Press.

Canedy, D. (2001, July 27). Florida teenager declares sorrow for killing teacher. *New York Times*, p. A12.

Card, C., ed. (1991). *Feminist ethics*. Lawrence: University of Kansas Press.

Childs, J. L. (1950/1967). *Education and morals: An experimentalist philosophy of education*. New York: John Wiley & Sons.

Chronicle of Higher Education (2001). Characteristics of recipient of doctorates, 1999. 48(1), 24.

Dantley, M. E. & N. H. Cambron-McCabe (2001, April). Licensure of Ohio school administrators and social justice concerns. Paper presented before the American Educational Research Association, Seattle, WA.

Dewey, J. (1910). *How we think*. Boston: D.C. Heath.

Dewey, J. (1910). *The influence of Darwin on philosophy*. New York: Holt.

Dewey, J. (1916). *Essays in experimental logic*. Chicago: University of Chicago Press.

Dewey, J. (1934). *Art as experience*. New York: Minton, Balch

Dewey, J. (1938). *Logic: The theory of inquiry*. New York: Holt.

Dewey, J. & J. H. Tufts (1908/1932). *Ethics* (rev. ed.). New York: Holt.

Duke, D. L. (1998). The normative context of organizational leadership. *Educational Administration Quarterly*, 34(2), 165–195.

English, F. W. (1992). *Educational administration: The human science*. New York: HarperCollins.

English, F. W. (1994). *Discourse and theory in educational administration*. New York: HarperColllins.

English, F. W. (2000, November). *De-constructing the 'right answers' to the SLLA (School Leaders Licensure Assessment): A snapshot on what counts for the 'correct' perspective and professional behavior in order to practice school administration.* Paper presented before the University Council for Educational Administration, Albuquerque, NM.

Fay, B. (1987). *Critical social science.* Ithaca, NY: Cornell University Press.

Ferguson, A. (1977). Androgyny as an ideal for human development. In M. Vetterling-Braggin, F. A. Elliston, & J. English (Eds.), *Feminism and philosophy.* Totowa, NJ: Littlefield, Adams.

Finn, C. E. Jr. (1991). *We must take charge: Our schools and our future.* New York: Free Press.

Fish, S. (1999). *The trouble with principle.* Cambridge, MA: Harvard University Press.

Fisher, B. & J. Tronto (1990). Toward a feminist theory of caring. In E. K. Abel & M. K. Nelson (Eds.), *Circles of care: Work and identity in women's lives.* Albany, NY: SUNY Press.

Flew, A. (1967). *Evolutionary ethics.* New York: St. Martin's Press.

Foster, W. P. (1986). *Paradigms and promises: New approaches to educational administration.* Buffalo, NY: Prometheus Books.

Foucault, M. (1967). *Madness and civilization.* London: Tavistock.

Fryer, M. (2001, July 15). St. James schools moving in right direction. *Sunday Advocate* (Baton Rouge, LA), p. 9B.

Fukuyama, F. (1995). *Trust: The social virtues and the creation of prosperity.* New York: Free Press.

Gilligan, C. (1982). *In a different voice: Psychological theory and women's development.* Cambridge, MA: Harvard University Press.

Giroux, H. (1988). *Schooling and the struggle for public life.* Minneapolis, MN: University of Minnesota Press.

Goodlad, J. (1984). *A place called school.* New York: McGraw-Hill.

Grimshaw, J. (1986). *Philosophy and feminist thinking.* Minneapolis, MN: University of Minnesota Press.

Hearn, F. (1997). *Moral order and social disorder: The American search for civil society.* New York: Aldine De Gruyter.

Hemsath, D. (2001). *301 more ways to have fun at work.* San Francisco, CA: Berrett-Koehler.

Hodgkinson, C. (1991). *Educational leadership.* Albany, NY: SUNY Press.

Hofstadter, R. (1970). *Social Darwinism in American thought.* New York: Beacon.

Hollingshead, A. (1949). *Elmtown's youth: The impact of social classes on adolescents.* New York: John Wiley & Sons, Inc.

House, E. R. (1994). Is John Dewey eternal? *Educational Researcher, 23*(1), 15–18.

Howard, P. K. (2001). *The lost art of drawing the line.* New York: Random House.

Hullfish, H. & P. G. Smith (1961). *Reflective thinking: The method of education.* New York: Dodd, Mead.

Huxley, T. H. (1896). *Evolution and ethics and other essays*. New York: D. Appleton.

Ingram, D. (1990). *Critical theory and philosophy*. New York: Paragon.

Interstate School Leadership Licensure Consortium (ISLLC) (1996). *Interstate School Leadership Licensure Consortium: Standards for School Leaders*. Washington, DC: Council of Chief State School Officers.

Jackson, P. W. (1998). *John Dewey and the lessons of art*. New Haven, CT: Yale University Press.

Jackson, P. W., R. Boostrum, & D. Hansen (1993). *The moral life of schools*. San Francisco: Jossey-Bass.

Keith, A. (1946). *Essays in human evolution*. London: Watts.

Keller, D. (1989). *Jean Baudrillard: From Marxism to postmodernism and beyond*. Stanford, CA: Stanford University Press.

Kohlberg, L. (1981). *Essays in moral development*. San Francisco: Harper & Row.

Lagemann, E. C. (2000). *An elusive science: The troubling history of education research*. Chicago: University of Chicago Press.

Lasch, C. (1984). *The minimal self*. New York: Norton.

Lefebvre, H. (1991). *The production of space*. (Donald Nicholson-Smith, Trans.). Oxford: Blackwell.

Levine, D. U. (1990). Update on effective schools: Findings and implications from research and practice. *Journal of Negro Education, 59*, 577–584.

Lightfoot, S. (1983). *The good high school: Portraits of character and culture*. New York: Basic Books.

Marshall, C. (2001, April). School administration licensure policy in North Carolina, 2001. Paper presented before the American Educational Research Association, Seattle, WA.

Marshall, C. (1992). *The assistant principal: Leadership choices and challenges*. Newbury Park, CA: Corwin.

Marshall, C., J. R. Steele, & D. L. Rogers (1993, April). *Caring as career: An alternative model for educational administration*. Paper presented at the annual meeting of the American Educational Research Association, Atlanta, GA.

Maxcy, S. J. (1991). *Educational leadership: A critical pragmatic perspective*. New York: Bergin & Garvey.

Maxcy, S. J. (1995). *Democracy, chaos, and the new school order*. Thousand Oaks, CA: Corwin.

Maxcy, S. J. (1998). Preparing school principals for ethno-democratic leadership. *International Journal of Educational Leadership, 1*(3), 217–235.

Maxcy, S. J. (2000, November). *The ethical standard, knowledge, and principal preparation*. Paper presented before the University Council for Educational Administration, Albuquerque, NM.

Maxcy, S. J., A. Tashakkori, & E. Iwanicki (1999, April). *Principal's perceptions regarding professional ethics: Importance and need for profes-*

sional development. American Educational Research Association, Montreal.

McCarthy, M. M., G. D. Kuh, L. J. Newel, & C. M. Iacona (1988). *Under scrutiny: The educational administration professoriate*. Tempe, AZ: University Council for Educational Administration.

McCarthy, M. M. & K. H. Murtadha (2001, April). *Standard-based certification for Indiana school leaders and social justice concerns*. Paper presented before the American Educational Research Association, Seattle.

McKerrow, K. (1997). Ethical administration: An oxymoron? *Journal of School Leadership, 7*, 210–225.

Mintzberg, H. (1973). *The nature of managerial work*. New York: Harper & Row.

Moore, G. E. (1903). *Principia ethica*. Cambridge: Oxford University Press.

Murry, J. H. Jr. (1995). *A study of the moral aspect of leadership in an urban school context*. Unpublished doctoral dissertation, University of New Orleans.

Murry, J. H., I. E. Bogotch, & L. F. Miron (1995, November). *Moral leadership practice within an urban context*. Paper presented before annual meeting of the Mid-South Educational Research Association, Biloxi, MS.

Nagel, T. (1999). Justice, justice, shalt thou pursue. *New Republic,* 1(423), 36–41.

Neville, R.C. (1989). Value, courage, and leadership. *Review of Metaphysics,* 43(1), 3–26.

Nietzsche, F. (1956). *The birth of tragedy and the genealogy of morals*. (F. Golffing, Trans.). Garden City, NJ: Doubleday.

Noddings, N. (1984). *Caring: A feminine approach to ethics and moral education*. Berkeley: University of California Press.

Pearsall, M. (Ed.). (1986). *Women and values: Readings in recent feminist philosophy*. Belmont, CA: Wadsworth.

Pigden, C. R. (1991). Naturalism. In Peter Singer (Ed.), *A companion to ethics* (pp. 421–431). Oxford: Blackwell, 421-431.

Purkey, S. & M. Smith (1982). Too soon to cheer? Synthesis of research on effective school. *Educational Leadership*, pp. 64–69.

Raup, R. B., G. Axtelle, K. Benne, & B. O. Smith (1943;1950). *The improvement of practical intelligence*. New York: Harper.

Rawls, J. (1972). *A theory of justice*. Oxford: Oxford University Press.

Richardson, V. (1990). The evolution of reflective teaching and teacher education. In R. T. Clift, W. R. Houston, & M. C. Pugach (Eds.), *Encouraging reflective practice in education* (pp. 3–19). New York: Teachers College Press.

Rorty, R. (1989). Achieving our country: Leftist thought in twentieth-century America. Cambridge, MA: Harvard University Press.

Rosenau, P. M. (1992). *Post-modernism and the social sciences*. Princeton, NJ: Princeton University Press.

Rouse, J. (1987). *Knowledge and power: Toward a political philosophy of science*. Ithaca, NY: Cornell University Press.

Roy, S. (1996). *The moral atmosphere of the elementary school and the question of gender*. Unpublished doctoral dissertation, Louisiana State University.

Sacks, P. (2001). *Standardized minds: The high price of America's testing culture and what we can do to change it*. New York: Perseus Books.

Schneewind, J. B. (1991). Modern moral philosophy. In P. Singer (Ed.), *A companion to ethics* (pp. 147–157). Oxford: Blackwell.

Schon, D. (1983). *The reflective practitioner*. New York: Basic Books.

Schon, D. A. (1990) The design process. In V. A. Howard (Ed.), *Varieties of thinking* (pp. 7–141). New York: Routledge.

Selznick, P. (1992). *The moral commonwealth*. Berkeley: University of California Press.

Sergiovanni, T. J. (1992). *Moral leadership: Getting to the heart of school improvement*. San Francisco: Jossey-Bass.

Sergiovanni, T. J. (1991). *The principalship: A reflective practice perspective* (2d ed.). Boston: Allyn & Bacon.

Simon, H. (1965). *Administrative behavior: A study of the decision making processes in administrative organizations* (2d ed.). New York: Free Press. (Original work published in 1947.)

Simon, H. (1971). *The sciences of the artificial*. Cambridge, MA: MIT Press.

Singer, P. (1979). *Practical ethics*. Cambridge, MA: Cambridge University Press.

Smith, A. G. R. (1972). *Science and society in the sixteenth and seventeenth centuries*. London: Harcourt Brace Jovanovich.

Smith, L. & J. H. M. Taylor (Eds). (1996). *Women and the book: Assessing the visual evidence*. London: British Library.

Starratt, R. J. (1994). *Building an ethical school: Practical response to the moral crisis in schools*. Philadelphia: Falmer Press.

Starratt, R. J. (1996). *Transforming educational administration: Meaning, community, and excellence*. New York: McGraw-Hill.

Staub, C. C. (1982). *Design process and communications: A case study* (2d ed.). Dubuque, IA: Kendall/Hunt.

Steffy, B. E. (1993). *The Kentucky education reform: Lessons for America*. Lancaster, PA: Technomic.

Strike, K. A., E. J. Haller, and J. F. Soltis (1998). *The ethics of school administration* (2d ed.). New York: Teachers College Press.

Strike, K. A. & P. L. Ternasky, (Eds.), (1993). *Ethics for professionals in education*. New York: Teachers College Press.

Sumner, W. G. (1963). *Social Darwinism: Selected essays*. (Introduction by Stow Persons). Englewood Cliffs, NJ: Prentice-Hall.

Swanstrom, T. (1993). Beyond economism: Urban political economy and the postmodern condition. *Journal of Urban Affairs*, 16(1), 55–78.

Tashakkori, A. & E. Iwanicki. (1998). Validation of the Louisiana Standards for Principals. Final project report, Louisiana Department of Education.

Taylor, C. (1989). *Sources of the self.* Cambridge, MA: Harvard University Press.

Turkle, S. (1995). *Life on the screen.* New York: Simon & Schuster.

Tyack, D. & E. Hansot (1982) Managers of virtue: Public school leadership in America, 1820–1980. New York: Basic Books.

Velleman, J. D. (1989). Practical Reflection. Princeton, NJ: Princeton University Press.

Vigil, J. (1988). *Barrio gangs: Street life and identity in Southern California.* Austin, TX: University of Texas Press.

Ward, L. F. (1883). *Dynamic Sociology, Or Applied Social Science, as Based Upon Statical Sociology and the Less Complex Sciences.* New York: D. Appleton and Co.

Westermarck, E. (1932). *Ethical relativity.* London: Kegan Paul, Trench, Trubner & Co. Ltd.

Whyte, W. F. (1943). *Street corner society: The social structure of an Italian slum.* Chicago: University of Chicago Press.

Williams, B. (1985). *Ethics and the limits of philosophy.* Cambridge, MA: Cambridge University Press.

Wilson, J. Q. (1993). The Moral Sense. New York: The Free Press.

Wilson, J. (1963). Thinking with concepts. Cambridge: Cambridge University Press.

Wolff, R. P. (1977). *Understanding Rawls.* Princeton, NJ: Princeton University Press.

Zeni, J., (ed.). 2001). *Ethical issues in practitioner research.* New York: Teachers College Press.

Index

About the Author

Spencer John Maxcy is author or editor of eleven books, has written over fifty book chapters and articles in journals, and presented numerous papers and symposia at scholarly conferences. Dr. Maxcy received the Ph.D. degree in History and Philosophy of Education from Indiana University and M.A. in History from Loyola University (Chicago). He is a Full Professor and Full Member of the Graduate Faculty at Louisiana State University, where he has taught for the past thirty years. His work focuses upon the application of pragmatism to the issues facing schools and educators, with particular reference to school leadership. His most recent work is a three volume set of John Dewey's works on education, reprinted with introductions and reviews, and published by Thoemmes Press in Great Britain.